The Financial System Explained:

What really happens when you swipe your card

Walter Bancroft

Walter Bancroft

Copyright 2024 Walter Bancroft. All Rights reserved. No part of this publication may be reproduced without the consent of the author.

"Money is a terrible master but an excellent servant."

~P.T. Barnum

Walter Bancroft

Table of Contents

Chapter 1: The Journey Begins—From Pocket to Purchase

Chapter 2: The Magic of the Swipe—Authorization Unveiled

Chapter 3: Beyond Authorization—Capturing and Settling Transactions

Chapter 4: The Digital Wallet Revolution

Chapter 5: Beyond Cards—Alternative Payment Methods

Chapter 6: Cryptocurrencies—The New Frontier

Chapter 7: Securing the Transaction—Fraud and Protection

Chapter 8: Regulations and Standards—The Rules of the Game

Chapter 9: Global Payments—Transactions Without Borders

Chapter 10: The Road Ahead—Innovations Shaping Payments

Introduction

Picture this: You tap your phone at your favorite coffee shop, and within seconds, your latte is paid for. It's a seamless transaction you probably don't think twice about. But have you ever wondered what actually happens in those few moments between tap and sip?

Welcome to "The Financial System Explained," where we'll unravel the hidden world behind your everyday purchases. In this book, we're going to lift the curtain on the intricate dance of digital dollars, revealing the unseen players and processes that make our modern financial world tick.

From the humble beginnings of bartering to the lightning-fast digital transactions of today, we've come a long way in how we exchange value. Yet, for many of us, the inner workings of these systems remain a mystery. That's about to change.

Throughout these pages, we'll break down complex concepts into bite-sized, easy-to-digest pieces. You'll discover how your money travels from your account to a merchant's, the security measures protecting your hard-earned cash, and the future innovations shaping our financial landscape.

Why does this matter? Because in our increasingly cashless society, understanding these systems isn't just interesting – it's essential. Knowledge is power, and in the realm of finance, it's the key to making smarter decisions, protecting yourself from fraud, and navigating the economic waters with confidence.

So, are you ready to decode the language of modern finance? To see the matrix behind every swipe, tap, and click? Let's begin our journey into the heart of the payment ecosystem – where technology meets money, and your coffee purchase is just the tip of the iceberg.

Walter Bancroft

Chapter 1: The Journey Begins—From Pocket to Purchase

The Evolution of Money

The story of money is as rich and diverse as the history of our civilization. It's a tale that flows through the rise and fall of empires, the changes in trade, and the always-shifting nature of trust. To grasp the complicated world of today's financial transactions, we need to look back through history, starting with the simple barter system that our early ancestors used.

Picture a world where people depended only on barter to get what they needed. If you had a goat and wanted a sack of grain, you had to find someone who had grain and was also interested in a goat. This tricky situation is what economists refer to as the "double coincidence of wants." The flaws of this system were obvious. You might have the best goat around, but if the farmer with the grain had just harvested a big crop, he wouldn't need your goat, leaving you with nothing but a bleating animal and an empty stomach.

While the barter system worked in small communities, it had many limitations. For one, it relied too much on mutual needs, which became a real headache as societies grew larger and more complex. With expanding trade routes and the development of more advanced civilizations, the need for a better way to exchange goods became clear. The shortcomings of barter highlighted the need for something that could represent value universally, and this set the stage for the evolution of money.

As societies advanced, certain items naturally emerged as suitable candidates for this new role. These commodity forms of money included valuable goods like gold, silver, and salt. The shiny appeal of gold made it especially attractive; not only was it beautiful, but it was also durable and easy to divide. Silver, with its own charm, offered a similar allure at a different value level. These items gained acceptance as currency, opening the door for more sophisticated economic interactions. Their worth came not just from their physical characteristics but also from a shared understanding within society that they had value.

This shift was a huge turning point in human history. People no longer had to chase down the farmer who had grain; they could now trade their gold or silver for whatever goods or services they wanted. The introduction of commodity money revolutionized trade, making transactions smoother and expanding the horizons of commerce. Imagine a bustling ancient marketplace where merchants swapped goods, and customers could easily satisfy their wants with a simple toss of a coin. This evolution led to another major advancement: the creation of coins.

The arrival of coinage was like a financial revolution. Governments began minting coins, marking them with symbols and images to show their authenticity and value. This system was no longer just about trust between individuals; it was based on a collective trust in the authority of the state to issue currency. The reliability of coins changed economies; it sped up trade, encouraged savings, and laid the groundwork for the complex financial systems we see today.

As societies became more intricate, so did their financial tools. The introduction of paper money during the medieval period marked another significant leap. While paper currency might seem flimsy compared to metal coins, it had many advantages. It was lighter and easier to carry, allowing for larger sums of money without the burden of heavy bags filled with coins. However, this change came with its own set of challenges, mainly centered around trust. Unlike coins that were physical and held intrinsic value, paper money depended entirely on the faith of its users. It was a promise from governments that the currency held value—essentially, a social contract.

This idea of trust became the foundation of our modern financial systems. Fiat money—currency issued by governments that isn't backed by a physical asset—depends on this social agreement. It is the trust in the issuing authority that gives paper money its worth. As societies moved into the industrial and global ages, this need for trust grew even stronger. The ability to conduct financial transactions without a tangible backing required individuals and businesses to take a leap of faith.

Now, as we look to the late 20th and early 21st centuries, we find ourselves on the brink of another significant transformation: the digital currency revolution. The rise of the internet has changed how people think about and use money. We're no longer limited by physical currency; we can now transfer value across the globe in an instant. Digital currencies like Bitcoin have introduced new ideas like decentralization and cryptography, which challenge traditional views of trust and authority in finance.

Bitcoin, the first cryptocurrency, uses a technology called blockchain. This innovative system records transactions across a network of computers, creating a secure, transparent ledger that can't be altered after the fact. This has huge implications for trust; instead of relying solely on governments or banks, users can trust the technology itself. The idea of a decentralized currency offers exciting possibilities for financial independence and security, but it also raises questions about regulation, stability, and the future of traditional banking.

When we reflect on the evolution of money, it's clear that the financial landscape is more than just a collection of ways to exchange goods. It's a living system shaped by human behavior, social needs, and technological advancements. From barter to digital currencies, each change has brought new challenges and opportunities. Understanding this history helps us appreciate the complexities of our current financial systems and empowers us to navigate them confidently.

In this ever-changing world of money, one thing remains constant: the need for a common medium of exchange. Whether it's a goat, a gold coin, a piece of paper, or a digital token, the core idea of facilitating trade and enabling economic interaction stays the same. As we move further into the digital age, our relationship with money will undoubtedly evolve, but the fundamental desire for connection, value, and trust will always be at the heart of every transaction. The journey of money reflects humanity's ongoing quest for efficiency, security, and understanding—a journey that will continue to unfold in ways we can only start to imagine.

Cash vs. Digital Payments

In a world that seems to be constantly on the move, the rivalry between cash and digital payments has become a major part of how we do business today. This shift isn't just about what's easier or what people prefer; it reflects how our society is changing alongside new technologies. As we explore this financial landscape, it's helpful to understand how traditional cash systems compare to the growing world of digital payments.

Recent statistics highlight the fact that cash use is dropping in many parts of the globe. A report from the Bank for International Settlements shows that cash transactions have significantly decreased in several developed countries, with many consumers now choosing electronic methods. For example, in Sweden, around 80% of transactions are made using cards or mobile payments. This change isn't unique to Sweden; countries like the UK, Canada, and Australia are seeing similar trends, where cash is becoming more of an afterthought than a primary way to pay. Infographics illustrating these shifts reveal the stark differences between the cash-dominated economies of the past and today's focus on digital solutions.

The growth of digital payments is closely tied to the technological advancements we've seen in recent years. Mobile wallets such as Apple Pay, Google Pay, and PayPal let people complete transactions with just a tap of their smartphones. Contactless technology has made it easy for consumers to pay simply by swiping their cards or devices over a reader. This convenience is a game-changer: there's no more digging through wallets or fumbling with change. Now, people can finish transactions almost effortlessly, making shopping a smoother experience.

Online banking has also played a big role in this shift. With just a few clicks, people can manage their finances, pay bills, and send money to friends and family—all from their homes. The pandemic sped up the use of these digital tools as people looked for safe, contactless ways to avoid germs. With more people shopping online, there was a corresponding rise in digital payment methods because consumers favored e-commerce platforms that minimized physical contact.

When we look at why people are moving toward digital payments, it's clear that convenience, security, and changes in lifestyle are key factors. Today's consumers want efficiency; they want to pay quickly and easily, fitting into a broader trend of wanting things right away. The simplicity of digital payment systems often outweighs the comfort or practicality that cash might bring. Security is another significant factor—digital payment systems often come equipped with advanced fraud protection features that cash simply doesn't offer. With the growing risk of theft or loss when carrying cash, many people feel more secure knowing their funds are safely stored digitally.

The impact of the pandemic is hard to ignore. As health concerns became a part of everyday life, many individuals started to avoid cash, viewing it as a potential source of germs. Retailers quickly adjusted to this change by offering contactless payment options, enabling customers to complete transactions without touching shared surfaces. This led to a significant push toward a cashless society. Surveys conducted during this time showed that many consumers were more willing to adopt digital payment methods, with a lot of them planning to continue using these options even after the pandemic.

However, as we dive deeper into this digital future, we can't overlook the challenges and limitations that cash still presents. While cash is a staple in many cultures, it comes with its own set of problems. Theft and loss are serious concerns for anyone who regularly carries cash, making it a less secure choice compared to digital methods. Plus, the physical nature of cash can create logistical issues, especially in a fast-paced world where speed and efficiency are prized. Having to handle cash transactions when instant payment is the norm can feel awkward, especially for those used to the immediacy of digital options.

The ease of carrying a credit card or using a smartphone is far more appealing than the bulk of coins and bills weighing down a wallet. Still, while people enjoy the convenience of digital transactions, they must also navigate the complexities of modern technology, which can include risks like data breaches and identity theft. Ironically, cash transactions often feel more straightforward and direct, while the digital realm introduces a layer of abstraction that can be unsettling for some.

This ongoing debate between cash and digital payments raises important questions about what money will look like in the future. Will cash eventually fade away, becoming a quaint relic of the past? Or will it remain a viable option for those who appreciate the physical aspect of currency? As we journey further into this unfamiliar territory, the choices we make as consumers will shape the future of payment systems.

While digital payments may be leading the way in today's commerce, it's crucial to keep in mind that cash still matters for many people and communities. Those living in rural areas with limited banking options often depend on cash for their everyday needs. Additionally, certain demographic groups, including the elderly or those without access to technology, are at a disadvantage in an increasingly digital world. Inclusivity and awareness of different perspectives are essential as we make this transition.

As society moves toward the ease of digital payments, it's important to remember the value of trust. Whether through cash or digital means, the core idea of money relies on the belief that it holds value. Digital currencies bring exciting new opportunities but also blur the lines of trust that have traditionally been established by banks and governments. Consumers are learning to place their faith in technology instead of institutions, leading to intriguing implications for the future of finance.

The evolution of payment systems reflects broader changes in society—our values, priorities, and our adaptability. The tension between cash and digital payments is about more than just money; it signifies cultural shifts that influence everything from economic inequality to our daily interactions. As we face these challenges, it's important to have meaningful conversations about the kind of payment systems we want and what they mean for our communities.

To wrap up this ongoing discussion, the coexistence of cash and digital payments highlights a fundamental truth about how we view money. Each method has its strengths and weaknesses, shaping how we conduct transactions and relate to one another. As we move forward, we need to find a balance that considers everyone's needs while embracing the innovations that digital payments bring. The future of money is being written right now, and as part of this evolving story, we all have the chance to influence the financial landscape for generations to come.

Your Role in the Payment Ecosystem: Understanding How Every Purchase Fits into a Larger System

When we think about money, it's easy to picture bills and coins, or maybe that online shopping spree that seemed like a good idea at the time. But buying something—whether it's a warm cup of coffee or the latest gadget—plays a much bigger role in the complex world of the payment ecosystem. Each purchase isn't just a simple exchange; it's a key part of a big, interconnected system that influences economies, affects industries, and touches our everyday lives. Grasping this idea is essential for anyone who wants to feel confident navigating the modern financial world.

Let's start with the idea that every transaction is part of a network that goes far beyond just exchanging goods for money. Each time you use your card or hit 'Buy Now,' you're stepping into a complex web that includes retailers, payment processors, banks, and even government regulations. This ecosystem isn't just a backdrop for our buying decisions; it's a living, breathing system that changes as technology develops, consumer habits evolve, and societal values shift. The combined actions of consumers like you and me fuel this system, influencing everything from market trends to inflation rates.

Now, let's take a look at what happens when you spend a dollar at a local café. Imagine you stroll into your favorite café and order a latte for $5. At first glance, it seems pretty straightforward: you pay, and you get your drink. But that latte's journey involves many different people. It starts with the coffee bean farmer, who grows the beans in distant lands and relies on a supply chain that includes shipping, processing, and distribution. The café owner has to juggle costs, wages, and overhead while making sure the business stays profitable, all while considering how the payment system affects pricing.

When you swipe your card or tap your phone to pay, the payment processor jumps into action, confirming your transaction in seconds. This involves several quick steps, like making sure you have enough money and that your payment method is valid. All of this happens in a flash, allowing you to enjoy your coffee without any hassle. But behind the curtain, countless systems are working hard to make this transaction smooth.

This connection highlights how important it is to understand your role as a consumer. Each decision you make—where to shop, what payment method to use, and how much to spend—has a ripple effect throughout the payment ecosystem. Choosing to support local businesses not only benefits your community but also boosts local economic health and job creation. The choice between cash and digital payments also reveals how comfortable you are with technology, how much you trust banks, and your awareness of security issues.

Furthermore, the rise of digital payments has added complexity that consumers need to navigate. Apps like Venmo, PayPal, and mobile wallets cater to different needs in the payment ecosystem, which can lead to varying consumer behaviors and expectations. For instance, the speed and convenience of mobile payments suit our desire for quick transactions, while cash payments might feel more traditional. In this way, your preferences and choices aren't just personal—they're part of a bigger story about consumer habits, how we embrace technology, and even economic patterns.

Let's also think about how outside factors can affect our buying habits. Economic conditions, technological innovations, and shifts in society all influence how we spend. For example, when times are tough, consumers might tighten their wallets, affecting everything from shopping habits to payment methods. On the flip side, during a booming economy, you might find yourself more willing to splurge, perhaps even jumping on the latest payment technologies that make spending easier and more appealing.

As we try to make sense of this complex ecosystem, keeping an eye on security and privacy is crucial. The convenience of digital payments has brought potential risks. With each transaction, you're trusting various parties—like retailers, banks, and payment processors—to keep your financial information safe, ensure your transactions are correct, and guard your money. But with constant headlines about data breaches and identity theft, it's important to stay alert and informed about how your data is managed and secured.

Finding the right balance between convenience and security is a key factor for today's consumers. Many people feel that the benefits of digital payments outweigh the risks, so they adopt these technologies without much hesitation. But others may prefer the tangibility of cash or more traditional payment methods. This difference in comfort levels shows how vital it is to understand where you fit into this ecosystem—not just as a buyer, but as someone who is informed and eager to protect your financial identity.

Your role goes beyond just individual purchases; it's also about grasping the broader economic impacts. Every time you buy something, you're tapping into your consumer power. This power can shape market trends, influence industries, and even hold companies accountable for their actions. For instance, many shoppers now prioritize sustainability, often looking for businesses that align with their values. This shift encourages companies to adopt more responsible practices, as those that don't may fall behind in a marketplace that increasingly values ethics.

Additionally, the rise of social media and online reviews has given consumers a voice like never before. You can share your experiences—good or bad—with a global audience in seconds. This ability to express your opinion can sway other people's buying decisions, create brand loyalty, or even drive customers away from businesses that don't meet their expectations. Therefore, your voice, combined with your spending habits, can have a significant impact on the payment ecosystem.

Moreover, loyalty programs and incentives have changed the shopping experience, adding another layer to consumer behavior. Many retailers use these programs to encourage customers to return, offering points for discounts or special offers. This tactic not only builds a sense of community among consumers but also influences their spending habits. People may find themselves leaning toward certain brands or stores, not just for the quality of products but for the rewards that come with their loyalty.

In this ecosystem, trust plays a crucial role. Trust in the financial institutions that manage payment systems, trust in the technologies that facilitate transactions, and trust in the brands we choose to support. With the emergence of digital currencies and blockchain technology, our understanding of trust is evolving. Consumers are beginning to place their faith in technology rather than traditional institutions, which has significant implications for finance's future.

As we embrace new advancements in payment systems, it's important to stay aware of how your actions shape this changing landscape. Each transaction isn't just about meeting a personal need; it's part of a bigger economic story. Recognizing this interconnectedness gives you the power to make choices that align with your values and priorities, fostering a meaningful relationship with money.

So, as you think about your place in this ecosystem, reflect on the broader impact of your purchasing decisions. The next time you swipe your card or tap your phone, remember that you're part of something much bigger. Your choices shape industries, influence market trends, and mirror the collective values of society. By staying informed and thoughtful, you can navigate the payment ecosystem with confidence and intention.

In the end, our relationship with money is changing alongside the payment systems we interact with. As technology progresses, the ways we conduct transactions will also evolve. However, the core principles of trust, choice, and connection will always remain. By embracing your role in this ecosystem, you become an active participant in shaping the future of finance, ensuring that your voice—and your choices—make a difference in the grand scheme of things. Your actions today can shape the landscape of tomorrow, and that's a powerful realization in the world of modern payments.

Walter Bancroft

Chapter 2: The Magic of the Swipe—Authorization Unveiled

What Happens When You Swipe

Have you ever thought about what really happens when you swipe your card at a payment terminal? It seems like such a simple action, something we do almost every day without thinking twice. But behind that quick movement lies a fascinating world of digital signals, financial agreements, and amazing technology. As cash fades into the background, getting to know how this process works can help us understand not just how our money moves, but also the clever systems that keep everything running smoothly.

Imagine standing at the checkout counter, surrounded by colorful products calling out to you from the shelves. You've filled your cart, and now, with a flick of your wrist, your card glides through the reader. Just like that, your purchase is done. But what happens in those few seconds after? Let's break it down into bite-sized pieces, just like slicing a cake into manageable servings.

The journey kicks off the moment you present your card to the terminal. As you swipe or tap, the terminal grabs your card info, including your card number, expiration date, and the all-important card verification value (CVV). This is a critical moment; the terminal reads the magnetic strip or, if you're using contactless payment, uses near-field communication to send your information to the payment processor. You can think of this as a secret handshake where specific data is exchanged at lightning speed.

Once the terminal gathers your details, it sends a request for authorization to the payment processor. Here's where the real magic happens. The processor acts like a busy traffic cop at a busy intersection, managing the flow of information. The request travels along a series of networks, which you can picture as a complex web of highways, each lane dedicated to sending data quickly and efficiently.

Next, the processor forwards the request to the card network—like a delivery service for your information. Card networks, such as Visa, MasterCard, or American Express, connect the merchant's acquiring bank to your issuing bank. They verify which bank issued your card and pass the request along to the right issuing bank.

Now, this is where things get serious. The issuing bank, your bank, receives the authorization request and starts checking things out. It looks at your account balance, checks for any signs of fraud, and confirms that your card is valid. It's like being at an exclusive club where the bouncer (the bank) makes sure you're on the guest list. Once the issuing bank is satisfied that everything is in order, it sends an approval or denial back through the same channels.

If everything goes smoothly, the issuing bank sends an authorization code back to the card network, which relays it to the processor and ultimately returns it to the merchant's terminal. If you could witness this process, you'd be amazed by how fast it all happens. What feels instantaneous to you is actually a beautifully orchestrated series of electronic exchanges, all occurring in just a few seconds.

But what if there's a hiccup? If the issuing bank spots a problem—like not enough money in your account or maybe your account is frozen due to suspicious activity—it will send back a denial code. The terminal then passes this information to the merchant, who might look at you with a confused expression, asking for another way to pay. It can be an awkward moment, even a bit embarrassing, but it's all part of the safety net designed to protect both you and the bank from potential fraud.

Once the transaction is approved, the merchant can wrap up the sale. However, the dance isn't over yet. Behind the scenes, the merchant's acquiring bank will talk to the issuing bank to settle the transaction, transferring the funds quickly from your bank to the merchant's account. This final step usually takes a couple of days, but it's an important part of the entire transaction process.

So, what may seem like a simple exchange between you and a merchant is actually a sophisticated system involving many players and transactions happening in the blink of an eye. Each step plays a crucial role in the larger machinery of payment systems, ensuring that our purchases get processed both efficiently and securely.

By diving deeper into this process, you'll discover the key players involved in this intricate dance of commerce and how their roles make the smooth experience we often don't think about possible. Understanding how card authorization works not only boosts our knowledge as consumers but also gives us the confidence to navigate the financial world. After all, when you swipe your card, you're not just making a purchase; you're taking part in a complex dance of technology, trust, and finance that has been refined over decades of innovation.

Meet the Key Players: Introducing the Cardholder, Merchant, Acquiring Bank, Issuing Bank, and Card Networks

To truly understand the dance of digital payments that happens every time we swipe a credit card, we need to get to know the important characters who keep this intricate process going. Like a great performance, the payment experience involves several essential players, each bringing their unique strengths to the table. From the cardholder who uses the card, to the merchant ready to accept payment, to the banks and networks making it all possible, recognizing these roles and how they work together will deepen our understanding of how we shop today.

Let's start with the cardholder, the face of this ecosystem. Picture a bustling coffee shop in a suburban neighborhood, where the rich scent of fresh coffee wafts through the air. In line, you'll see a mix of customers—some digging through their bags for loose change, while others confidently swipe their shiny credit or debit cards at the checkout. This choice, favoring plastic over cash, marks a big shift in how people prefer to pay.

The cardholder is a key player in this whole process, and often doesn't even think about the perks that cards offer. The biggest draw? Convenience. With just a quick flick of the wrist, someone can finish a purchase without the hassle of counting coins or waiting for change. As our lives get busier, being able to make a payment quickly isn't just a nice perk; it's become an expectation. Plus, many people are attracted to rewards programs that turn everyday purchases into opportunities to earn points, travel miles, or cash back.

But the cardholder's impact goes beyond just personal choices and immediate rewards. The way they use their cards helps shape spending trends and provides valuable information for merchants and banks alike. For example, during the pandemic, there was a noticeable rise in contactless payments driven by health concerns and a desire for less physical contact. This shift pushed merchants to quickly update their payment systems, showing how responsive this entire ecosystem can be to what consumers want.

Now, let's turn to the merchant—the next major player in this financial story. Imagine the busy owner of a charming local bakery, who has poured countless hours, money, and effort into creating a warm space filled with delicious treats. This merchant isn't just selling goods; they are a vital part of the local economy. Merchants come in all shapes and sizes, from cozy coffee shops and grocery stores to huge online platforms like Amazon. No matter where they fit in, every merchant has the same crucial task: accepting payments efficiently while keeping their systems safe.

For merchants, deciding to accept card payments usually comes down to wanting to reach more customers. Many shoppers prefer the ease and speed of card transactions nowadays. However, this convenience doesn't come without challenges. Accepting card payments means dealing with a maze of regulations, processing fees, and security issues. Merchants must find a careful balance between making it easy for customers to pay and protecting their sensitive financial information.

The bond between merchants and their acquiring banks is a big part of this picture. The acquiring bank acts like a trusted guide, helping merchants navigate the complicated world of payment processing. This bank handles the transactions that happen when a cardholder swipes their card, elevating the request to the higher levels of the financial network, and ultimately connecting it to the issuing bank.

An acquiring bank wears many hats—it provides the tech merchants need, helps with compliance issues, and ensures that money flows smoothly from customers to businesses. They also educate merchants on security measures to guard against fraud and data breaches, which can be both damaging and costly. In a world where data breaches happen all too often, merchants have to stay alert, and their vigilance often relies on the support of their acquiring bank.

Next up is the issuing bank, the powerhouse that drives consumer spending. When someone applies for a credit card, it's the issuing bank that checks their creditworthiness, sets their spending limit, and manages their account. This is the bank that ultimately decides if a transaction gets approved or denied.

Picture a scenario where a shopper, excited to buy a new gadget online, enters their card details. The issuing bank jumps into action, checking the transaction against a series of criteria. Do they have enough funds available? Has anything suspicious been flagged on the account? This vital gatekeeping role means that the issuing bank not only influences how much someone can spend but also works to protect their interests by spotting and preventing fraud.

Besides approving transactions, issuing banks also offer real-time customer service. If a cardholder loses their card or thinks there's been fraudulent activity, it's the issuing bank they call for help. They've become a reassuring presence, ready to lend support during stressful moments. These banks also play a part in helping consumers understand their spending habits and manage their finances, often through user-friendly apps and online tools that provide insights into their spending patterns.

Finally, we come to the card networks, the backbone of the payment process. Think of them as the vast highways that enable the flow of transactions between merchants and banks. Networks like Visa, MasterCard, and American Express connect everything, ensuring transactions happen smoothly and securely.

These networks set the rules for how transactions are handled, how fees are shared, and how disputes are resolved. They act as the link between acquiring banks and issuing banks, making sure that information flows without interruptions. Without these networks, the delicate process of payment handling would come to a standstill.

Moreover, card networks are key players in maintaining security. They constantly invest in new technologies designed to protect both consumers and merchants from fraud, like encryption and tokenization. Their role in keeping trust in the payment system strong can't be overstated; if consumers didn't feel secure about card transactions, many would likely revert to cash or other less reliable payment methods.

As we take a step back and look at how these players interact—the cardholder, merchant, acquiring bank, issuing bank, and card networks—we see that each part is crucial for the success of cashless transactions. This process isn't just a series of disconnected actions; it's a well-choreographed performance where each person has a specific role to fulfill.

Understanding these roles helps us see the larger picture of the payment ecosystem. It allows us to appreciate the complexity behind our everyday transactions, turning what seems like a simple swipe into a detailed operation that connects technology, finance, and consumer habits. This knowledge empowers us as consumers to navigate the financial landscape with greater confidence, enabling informed choices about how we spend our money in a world that's increasingly moving away from cash.

Security Measures in a Split Second: Learning How Fraud is Prevented During Authorization

In the hustle and bustle of our daily lives, we often take the security of our financial information for granted. But behind the scenes, a clever web of technologies and processes works hard to keep our sensitive data safe. Picture this: you walk into a busy café, place your order, and pay with a quick swipe or tap of your card. What feels like a simple action is actually a complex dance of security measures designed to make sure this transaction is as secure as possible.

From the moment you swipe your card to when the payment goes through, a series of important security steps kick into action. One of the first lines of defense is encryption, which can be thought of like the secret codes used by spies. Imagine two friends chatting at a café, sharing secrets in a language only they understand. Just as they keep their conversation private, encryption scrambles your card information into a code that only trusted parties can read. This way, if a bad actor tries to intercept your data while it's being sent, they'll only find a jumbled mess of letters and numbers that is useless to them. This process not only safeguards your data but also helps build trust in the payment system; after all, who wants to engage in transactions if they think their information could be easily stolen?

Next up is tokenization, which is a really interesting concept that replaces your sensitive card details with a unique identifier, or "token." Let's say you're at an amusement park. When you buy a ticket, you receive a wristband or token that gives you access to rides, but it's not the cash value of the ticket itself. Tokenization works the same way; your actual credit card number is switched out for a temporary token that can only be used for that one transaction. If someone managed to get a hold of this token, they still wouldn't be able to access your card details, greatly lowering the chances of fraud.

The beauty of tokenization is that it keeps the actual value of your transaction hidden, making the payment process smoother while protecting you from potential theft. This method is vital in today's digital economy, where data breaches happen all too often. Security measures like tokenization aren't just tech jargon; they represent a big change in how we think about financial transactions.

Now, let's bring machine learning and artificial intelligence into the picture, which are quickly becoming the protectors of our online wallets. Imagine a watchful guard at the entrance of a fancy casino, keeping an eye on every visitor. That's exactly what machine learning algorithms do. They study transaction patterns and spot anything unusual that might suggest fraud, all in real time.

For example, think about a cardholder who usually buys things in their local area but suddenly tries to make a large purchase thousands of miles away. The machine learning models, trained on huge sets of data, would catch this odd behavior and send up a red flag for potential fraud. This quick response can prevent unauthorized transactions before they happen, stopping unwanted charges in their tracks.

This proactive monitoring isn't just a backup plan; it's like a finely tuned orchestra playing in harmony. The algorithms constantly learn and adapt to new types of fraud, getting better at identifying what's legitimate and what's suspicious. They sift through a mountain of data, spotting trends and insights that no human could manage on their own at such a large scale. This ongoing watchfulness is what keeps modern transaction security strong, giving consumers the confidence to shop, eat out, and travel without worry.

Understanding payment security also means knowing the various rules that guide how transactions are processed. One of the key players here is the Payment Card Industry Data Security Standard (PCI DSS). Think of PCI DSS as the regulatory authority in the digital transaction world, making sure that everyone—merchants, banks, and card networks—follows strict rules to minimize the chances of data breaches.

The heart of PCI DSS isn't just about regulations; it creates a standard approach to keeping data safe that builds trust with consumers. When merchants stick to these guidelines, shoppers can feel reassured that their financial information is being looked after properly. This is especially important now that digital payments have become as common as sending a text message. Knowing there's a regulatory framework in place gives us an extra layer of protection.

However, the payment security world is always changing, often keeping pace with the cleverness of fraudsters. As we look ahead, several new technologies are set to offer even stronger protections for our financial transactions. One exciting area is biometrics, which is gaining popularity as a smart security measure. Imagine using your fingerprint or facial recognition to identify yourself when you make a purchase. This technology could make traditional PINs and passwords outdated, providing a smoother and more secure experience.

Additionally, the growth of blockchain technology opens up new possibilities. By decentralizing transaction records, blockchain offers a secure and unchangeable ledger that could cut down on fraud risks and data tampering. The transparency and traceability of blockchain systems could add another layer of security, helping consumers feel even safer as they manage their finances.

As consumers, it's important for us to stay alert in this rapidly evolving landscape. While technology advances in security, our individual responsibility is key to protecting our personal information. Regularly checking account statements, using strong and unique passwords, and being careful about where and how we share information are all essential steps that help us take charge of our financial security.

Moreover, education is a valuable tool on this journey. By learning about the ways our financial information is protected and recognizing the roles of encryption, tokenization, and machine learning, we can feel empowered. Understanding the regulations that support payment security helps us appreciate the many safeguards in place, creating a more informed group of consumers who can confidently navigate the world of transactions.

In this complex ecosystem, the teamwork between technology, regulation, and consumer awareness builds a solid framework for safety. The ongoing battle against fraud reflects the dynamic world we live in, where technology serves as both a tool and a shield. As we embrace cashless transactions, understanding and respecting the details of security will help us adapt and succeed in this modern financial landscape.

So, the next time you swipe your card or tap to pay, remember that behind that simple action is a whole world of security measures working tirelessly to keep you safe. From encryption to tokenization and the ever-watchful machine learning, these advancements not only boost our shopping experiences but also nurture a culture of trust within the financial system. It's this blend of technology, regulation, and consumer awareness that creates a protective shield, ensuring our finances stay secure in an increasingly digital world.

Walter Bancroft

Chapter 3: Beyond Authorization—Capturing and Settling Transactions

The End-of-Day Ritual: Discovering What Happens When Merchants Close Their Registers

As the sun sets, painting the bustling streets in soft colors, merchants get ready to close their registers after a long day. This end-of-day ritual is something many of us may not think much about—a whirlwind of activity characterized by cash drawers opening and closing, the beep of barcode scanners, and the relieved sighs from staff who have weathered another busy day in retail. But as the visible hustle and bustle settles, there's a crucial process happening behind the scenes that many don't see when they swipe their cards or tap their phones to pay.

Once the last shopper leaves and the store lights dim to a cozy glow, merchants finally take a breath. Yet, their work doesn't just end with a polite 'thank you' and a wave goodbye. They dive into an important phase that ensures the money we spent makes its way into their accounts. This isn't just about tallying up daily sales; it's the start of a complex journey where our money travels from our pockets into the hands of the merchants.

What makes this process so interesting is how precise it is. When merchants close their registers, they carefully record the day's sales—each transaction is a vital piece of their business puzzle. There's a special satisfaction in watching those numbers grow, reflecting all the hard work that went into the day. Yet, what happens after that can feel like a mystery, often wrapped in the confusing language of finance and banking.

Once the numbers are tallied, the real action begins. This is where clearing and settlement come into play. Clearing, simply put, is a preparation stage that ensures all the transaction details are checked and ready for the final transfer. This step makes sure the funds are available and that everything is on the up and up, offering protection to both the merchant and the consumer.

Picture the busy highways of a city—each lane represents a different transaction. Just as cars must navigate through traffic lights, merges, and tolls to get where they're going, financial transactions have their own routes through various banks and networks. As our money travels, it gets examined, verified, and approved, moving smoothly from one account to the next, but not without those necessary checks along the way.

After the clearing process is done, we move into the realm of settlement. This is where the real magic happens—the actual transfer of funds. Think of it like the grand finale of a fireworks show; all the buildup leads to this moment when everything explodes in color. In financial terms, settlement is the point when the merchant's bank receives the money, and the consumer's account is debited. It wraps up all those intricate steps that started with a simple card swipe.

But the journey doesn't end at settlement. From when a transaction gets approved to when the merchant finally sees the cash in their account, many factors can influence how fast and smoothly this process goes. Time is of the essence, and every second matters. Merchants, eager to see the rewards of their hard work, often find themselves anxiously waiting for their revenue to show up in their accounts.

As the night goes on and the staff completes their paperwork, they might think about how vital this end-of-day ritual is. It's a key moment in the life of a transaction that helps the business run efficiently. Closing the register isn't just a routine; it opens up a window into understanding how the financial world operates behind the scenes of shopping.

For merchants, this end-of-day ritual allows them not only to balance their sales but also to reflect on how the day went. Each time they close the register, they gain insights into customer behavior, trends, and preferences. Maybe they notice that some products sold out while others barely moved, prompting them to rethink their stock and marketing plans for the future.

This kind of reflection is essential for adapting and growing in an ever-changing market. It's a dance between instinct and numbers, where understanding those figures leads to smart decisions. This ritual encourages a mindset of constant improvement, helping merchants sharpen their operations and better meet their customers' needs.

As the final reports print and the cash drawer clicks shut, the financial world continues its quiet hum in the background. The money is already on its way, traveling through the complex network of payment processors, banks, and financial institutions, all working together to ensure everything goes off without a hitch. Each player in this system is crucial, harmonizing their efforts to make this seemingly simple act of purchasing happen.

For consumers, all these processes are often hidden, masked by the ease of technology. We tap, swipe, and click without giving it much thought, assuming our transactions will smoothly move from our accounts to those of the merchants. However, understanding the behind-the-scenes work can help us appreciate the systems that keep our cashless society running.

When we think about this end-of-day ritual, it becomes clear that closing a register marks the start of a bigger story—a story filled with checks and balances, where every step is designed to protect and serve everyone involved. It highlights the sophistication of today's payment systems, where countless transactions come together in a seamless flow of money that supports businesses and economies.

So, the next time you're making a purchase, take a moment to consider the journey your money is taking. From the warmth of the cash register to the intricate machinery of banking, every transaction has its own story. It's a story of trust, verification, and the endless quest for efficiency in a world that never stops moving. When merchants close their registers, they're not just shutting down for the night; they're part of a financial dance that happens quietly behind the scenes, making our cashless transactions possible.

Clearing vs. Settlement: Differentiating Between These Crucial Backend Processes

In the world of financial transactions, two terms often come up and create some confusion: clearing and settlement. Both of these processes play vital roles each time you buy something, but they each have their own specific jobs that are important for making payment systems run smoothly. To make things clearer, let's use some relatable examples to break down these concepts into simpler terms.

Imagine clearing as a busy mailroom sorting through letters and packages, while settlement is like the actual delivery of those sorted items to their final destinations. If you can picture that, you're already on the right path.

First, let's talk about clearing. This is the step where transaction details are shared between two banks: the issuing bank, which is your bank, and the acquiring bank, which is the merchant's bank. For example, when you swipe your credit card at a café to grab your morning coffee, that action kicks off the clearing process. Think about a crowded mailroom where stacks of letters and packages are getting organized. Similarly, transaction details from your coffee purchase are sent to the right financial institutions. Your bank checks to make sure you have enough money to pay for your coffee and that your card hasn't been reported lost or stolen. Meanwhile, the merchant's bank gets ready to receive this information.

At this point, you can think of the transaction details as packages waiting to be processed. They require careful coordination among various financial institutions. Just like a mailroom worker sorts mail by zip code and address to ensure it reaches the right place, banks go through a detailed process of verifying transaction details and figuring out how much money needs to be cleared between them. The beauty of clearing lies in its ability to handle many transactions at once—imagine a well-running assembly line where each piece has to fit perfectly to guarantee everything works efficiently.

Now, imagine a bustling downtown café that serves hundreds of customers every day, each one swiping their cards for their caffeine fix. The café's acquiring bank gathers all these transaction details throughout the day, getting everything ready for processing. This is where clearing really shines. Each transaction gets processed in groups, allowing banks to manage the volume smoothly. After everything is cross-checked and confirmed, the clearing phase comes to an end, making way for the next step.

Now let's move on to settlement, the next part of this financial journey. Once clearing is complete and all transaction details are verified, we reach the point where the actual transfer of funds happens. Think of settlement as the moment when those neatly sorted packages are loaded onto delivery trucks on their way to their destinations. This is where the real action takes place—the money moves from your account to the merchant's bank account.

The settlement process involves several steps, beginning with netting. This is where the banks balance out the amounts they owe each other based on all the transactions. Let's say that by the end of the day, all the coffee purchases at our café add up to $1,000. The acquiring bank must now settle this amount with the issuing banks. The netting process helps cut down on the number of transactions that need to be settled, making everything more efficient.

After the banks have netted the transactions, they move on to the actual debit and credit actions. Your account is debited for what you spent, while the café's account gets credited with that amount. Here's the interesting part: while clearing often happens almost instantly after you make a purchase, settlement can take days to complete, depending on the payment method and the agreements between banks.

To highlight the differences, let's look at a few common payment methods: credit cards, debit cards, and digital wallets. Each of these has its own unique clearing and settlement timelines, which showcases the complexity behind seemingly simple transactions.

When you use a credit card, the clearing happens quickly, sometimes in just seconds. The transaction gets verified, and the funds are authorized, but the settlement might take several days. Credit card networks typically settle transactions at the end of each day or at specific points during the week. The merchant may see the funds in their account within 1-3 business days, depending on the card network and agreements. It's like getting a package delivered a few days after it's left the mailroom.

On the other hand, debit card transactions usually settle faster. When you use a debit card, the funds typically transfer almost immediately from your checking account to the merchant's account. It's similar to a same-day delivery service, where sorted packages are quickly dispatched right after being organized. Consumers often feel this quick turnaround because the money leaves their account as soon as the transaction is approved.

Digital wallets add another layer to the clearing and settlement process. When you pay using a mobile wallet like Apple Pay or Google Pay, it goes through a clearing process similar to credit cards, but it can be faster thanks to the technology involved. However, the settlement process can vary greatly depending on the wallet provider and the merchant's bank. In some cases, digital wallets can allow for instant settlements, letting merchants access their funds almost right away. It's as if those packages have been pre-sorted and zoomed off to their destinations in no time.

With these examples in mind, it's clear that even though consumers often enjoy a smooth transaction experience, there's a complex dance happening behind the scenes. Most people may not think about the ins and outs of clearing and settlement, but these processes are what ensure that every swipe of a card, every tap of a phone, and every completed purchase is handled with great care.

This intricate balance of clearing and settlement doesn't just help individual transactions; it also supports the larger financial system. Banks, payment processors, and merchant service providers work together to manage risks, follow regulations, and keep consumer trust. By having strong systems in place for clearing and settlement, these financial institutions help reduce fraud and operational risks, creating a safe environment for cashless transactions.

In short, clearing and settlement are two sides of the same coin—both crucial for making payments work smoothly but different in what they do and how long they take. As consumers, we might overlook these processes, focusing mainly on the convenience of cashless transactions. However, understanding the mechanics behind clearing and settlement helps us appreciate the sophisticated systems that allow us to make everyday purchases.

So next time you swipe your card for that morning latte or tap your phone at the grocery store, take a moment to recognize the behind-the-scenes efforts that make it all happen. The flow of money from your account to the merchant's bank isn't just a coincidence; it's the result of a carefully managed process involving clearing, settlement, and a variety of financial players working together to ensure that transactions run smoothly and securely. It's a financial dance—a choreography of precision and timing that supports the cashless society we navigate each day.

How Merchants Get Paid: Following the Money From Your Account to the Merchant's Bank

In today's world of digital payments, making a purchase can feel like magic. One moment you're in a busy coffee shop, eagerly waiting for your latte, and the next you're tapping your card or smartphone on the reader. Just like that, money is transferred from your account to the merchant's bank, creating a smooth and almost instant experience. However, behind this simplicity lies a complicated web of people, processes, and technologies that work together to make sure everything goes off without a hitch.

To really understand how money moves from your account to the merchant's bank, let's picture the journey of those funds in our minds. Imagine a flowchart hanging up in a bustling operations room. At the top, we have the consumer—let's call her Sarah. Sarah steps into her favorite café, ready to enjoy her daily coffee. As she reaches for her card, a series of actions kicks into gear, with various players collaborating to make her payment happen.

First up is the payment gateway, which is like a friendly barista taking orders at the counter. This system securely captures Sarah's payment information and sends it off to the payment processor. Think of the processor as the café's kitchen—this is where all the behind-the-scenes work takes place. The processor is in charge of confirming the transaction and checking that Sarah has enough money in her account for her latte. If everything looks good, the processor sends the information back to the payment gateway, which then alerts the coffee shop's payment system that the transaction is approved.

Now, let's pause and get a closer look at the key players involved in this complex transaction. The payment processor is crucial in connecting different financial institutions to help move the money. It acts as the link between the merchant's bank (called the acquirer) and Sarah's bank (known as the issuer). Just like a conductor leading an orchestra, the payment processor ensures that all the players communicate effectively and in harmony.

The acquirer is the merchant's bank, similar to the café owner taking care of all the financial matters. This bank manages the café's account and is responsible for receiving the funds transferred from the issuer after Sarah buys her coffee. On the other hand, the issuer is Sarah's bank—the one that holds her money. Its role is to verify whether Sarah has enough funds to buy her latte and if her card is valid.

As Sarah swipes her card, the authorization process kicks off. It's like she's sending a quick message to her bank saying, "I'd like to buy this latte, please!" The bank gets the request, checks everything, and replies with either an approval or a denial. If the bank gives the green light, the money doesn't leave Sarah's account just yet; it's simply put on hold for the purchase. This part of the process usually happens in a flash, reassuring Sarah that she can enjoy her drink.

Once authorization is completed, the transaction details move on to clearing. Here's where the earlier "mailroom" analogy comes into play. All the transaction details are organized and exchanged between the banks, ensuring the right amounts are taken from Sarah's account and credited to the café. It's a busy hub of activity, where lots of transactions are processed together, making everything run efficiently.

After clearing, we enter the settlement phase, which is when the funds actually move. Picture the café owner eagerly waiting for the money from the day's sales. After the banks reconcile all the transactions, the real debiting and crediting occur. Sarah's bank takes the money from her account for the latte, while the café's bank receives the deposit, completing the sale.

But how long does it take for Sarah's favorite coffee shop to get its money? The timing can vary for a few reasons, like whether the transaction was in-person or online, and the relationship between the merchant and their bank. Generally, in-person purchases like Sarah's can result in funds showing up in the merchant's account within one to three business days. Online transactions might take longer because of the extra steps needed to verify shipping and prevent fraud.

Some merchants have special arrangements with their banks that let them access their money almost immediately. Imagine if Sarah's café had a special deal with their bank that allowed them to get paid right away. It would be like receiving instant cash back, keeping the business running without a hitch.

Now, let's circle back to Sarah as she enjoys her latte. With every sip, she might not think about the intricate network that made that moment happen. From her initial swipe to the café getting its funds, a whole system of players and processes works behind the scenes to ensure that every payment goes smoothly. It's an amazing journey that highlights the complexities of our modern financial world.

While the ease of cashless transactions might lead us to forget the details involved, understanding how money flows in these situations helps us appreciate the technology and systems that support our everyday lives. The next time you swipe your card for that latte or tap your phone to pay for groceries, take a moment to think about the fascinating journey the money takes. It doesn't just disappear; it travels through various checkpoints and players before reaching its final stop.

As consumers in a cashless society, knowing how these processes work gives us more confidence in our financial decisions. By understanding the journey of money and the roles of payment gateways, processors, and banks, we become better informed. Whether it's paying for coffee or booking a vacation, the intricate web of transactions helps keep commerce flowing in our world. So go ahead, enjoy that latte, knowing there's a whole economic engine working behind the scenes to make it happen.

Walter Bancroft

Chapter 4: The Digital Wallet Revolution

Mobile Payments Explained: Unpacking How Apple Pay, Google Pay, and Others Work

Picture this: It's a busy Monday morning, and you walk into a café with your hands full—maybe you're juggling a briefcase, a laptop bag, and even a steaming cup of coffee. As you approach the register, the last thing you want is the hassle of digging through your wallet for cash or a credit card. Instead, with a quick double-click of your smartphone's side button and a flick of your thumb, you're ready to pay. The barista glances at your screen, nods, and just like that, you're off again, already thinking about your next meeting. This little moment isn't just about convenience; it showcases how mobile payments have changed the way we handle money.

At the core of mobile payments are digital wallets—apps that let you store your payment information safely and make transactions without a hitch. Services like Apple Pay, Google Pay, and Samsung Pay have shaken up the financial landscape, allowing folks to leave their bulky wallets behind and rely on their smartphones for everyday purchases. The technology behind these apps is both fascinating and intricate, involving clever tricks like encryption, tokenization, and near-field communication (NFC).

So, how does it all work? When you use a mobile payment app, the first step is connecting your bank account or credit card to the service. This is usually pretty simple; you just enter your card info into the app. What happens next is pretty smart: instead of storing your actual card details, the app transforms them into a unique identifier called a token. This token acts like a shield for your sensitive information, so your real card number is never shared during transactions. When you tap your phone on a compatible payment terminal, it's this token that gets sent, not your credit card number—pretty clever, right? It's all about keeping your data safe from potential fraud.

Now, let's talk about speed. The whole process is incredibly quick. Once your token is sent to the merchant's payment processor, it gets verified against the original data stored securely by your bank. Your bank checks for anything suspicious—like not having enough funds or signs of fraud—before giving the thumbs up for the transaction. This all happens in just a few seconds, making for a smooth checkout experience. It almost feels like magic, thanks to a well-oiled network of banks and payment processors working tirelessly behind the scenes.

One of the biggest perks of mobile payments is how convenient they are. In a world where we all crave instant results, being able to make a purchase with a few taps gives you control over your spending. No more scrambling for loose coins or straining your eyes in a dimly lit restaurant to figure out your bill. With mobile payments, buying things is not only faster; it's also easier to keep track of your spending. Most digital wallet apps keep a detailed history of your purchases, helping you budget and manage your finances better.

But let's not forget that convenience comes with its own set of challenges. As more people start using mobile payments, the need for consumer education becomes important. Many folks are still hesitant about jumping in, often worried about security. Questions swirl around whether their personal info is safe or if they could recover their funds if something goes wrong. To help ease these worries, the companies behind these services have poured a lot into strong security measures, including encryption, biometric authentication, and real-time fraud detection systems to keep users protected.

It's also crucial for users to know that mobile payments aren't entirely risk-free. If your phone goes missing or gets stolen, there's a chance for unauthorized transactions, even with safety measures in place. Most apps require biometric verification—like a fingerprint or facial recognition—before you can make any payments, but the possibility of someone gaining access isn't completely off the table. So, it's equally essential to learn how to secure your mobile device as it is to know how to use a digital wallet.

Another issue on the horizon for mobile payments is the digital divide. While cities might boast top-notch payment technology, many rural areas still struggle with slow internet and outdated point-of-sale systems. This gap in digital payment access raises questions about inclusivity. As digital wallets gain traction, it's important for everyone involved to consider how to ensure these payment systems are available to all, no matter where they live or their income level.

Despite these hurdles, the future of mobile payments looks promising, with ongoing tech advancements set to push the digital wallet revolution even further. Innovative ideas like blockchain technology and artificial intelligence could change the payment game entirely. Blockchain, for instance, offers a new way of processing transactions that could boost security and transparency. At the same time, AI could lead to personalized payment solutions that adapt to our own spending habits, making transactions even smoother.

As we look ahead, the growth of digital wallets isn't just about making things more convenient; it also signals a shift in how we think about money. With mobile payments on the rise, we might start relying less on traditional banking and cash transactions. Businesses could benefit from faster payment processing, while consumers might enjoy better rewards programs tailored to their spending styles.

Furthermore, as more people start using digital wallets, we might see a change in how we shop. The ease of making purchases could lead to more impulse buying, which could change how we budget and manage our money. This shift poses important questions for businesses, too. Retailers will have to adapt to this new world of commerce, rethinking how they connect with customers and tweaking their payment systems to cater to digital wallets.

Ultimately, the rise of mobile payments represents a major change in how we relate to money. As digital wallets become an everyday part of our lives, it's vital to balance the benefits of convenience and security with the need for access and education. By exploring how platforms like Apple Pay and Google Pay work, we gain a better grasp of this digital landscape—one that keeps evolving and reshaping how we interact with our finances. As we move forward, the possibilities are vast, limited only by how open we are to adapting to these new payment solutions.

NFC Technology: Understanding the Tech That Enables Contactless Payments

Imagine stepping into a lively coffee shop, where soft music fills the air and the wonderful smell of freshly brewed coffee surrounds you. After some thoughtful consideration about whether to try that new seasonal drink or stick with your favorite, you finally make your choice. As you head to the counter to pay, instead of rummaging through your bag for cash or a credit card, you simply bring your smartphone close to the payment terminal. You hear a cheerful beep and see a reassuring green light flash—just like that, you're done! This smooth experience is thanks to a quiet hero in the world of payments: Near Field Communication, or NFC technology.

At its heart, NFC is a short-range wireless communication technology that lets devices share information when they're just a few centimeters apart. Picture it as two friends standing close together, sharing secrets without anyone else listening in. When you tap your smartphone to make a payment, it's like that private exchange—just with no words spoken. It's a quick and efficient method of communication, making it perfect for contactless payments.

So, how does this technology actually work? Let's break it down into simpler parts. When you decide to make a contactless payment, your smartphone creates a unique radio signal. This signal is sent to the payment terminal as you bring your phone near it. The terminal picks up this signal, understands it, and finishes the transaction in just seconds. This is possible because of a mix of RFID (Radio Frequency Identification) and NFC technology, which allows data to move quickly without needing any physical connections. Imagine passing a note to a friend; instead of handing over paper, you're sending data with a swift gesture.

The way an NFC transaction works is both simple and fascinating. First, your payment app securely keeps your payment information safe through encryption. When you tap your phone on the terminal, it sends a token representing your payment information instead of your actual card details. Think of this token as a digital stand-in that allows the payment to happen without exposing sensitive information. The payment terminal and your bank check in with each other to confirm the transaction, making sure you have enough funds and that everything looks okay. If all goes well, the transaction gets the green light, and you're on your way. This all happens in the blink of an eye, making the payment experience easy and enjoyable for many people.

One of the biggest perks of NFC technology is speed. In our busy lives, being able to make payments in just a few moments can really make a difference. Traditional payment methods—whether cash or card—often involve several steps, like digging through your wallet, inserting a card, waiting for the terminal to process, and sometimes signing a receipt. But with NFC, all of that fuss is replaced by a simple tap. This extra efficiency can be especially helpful in crowded retail spaces, where long lines can frustrate customers and cost sales. By using NFC-enabled payment systems, businesses not only improve the customer experience but also boost their operational efficiency.

The benefits of NFC technology go beyond just speed; they touch on another important issue that many people care about these days: cleanliness. Since the COVID-19 pandemic, more folks are thinking about the surfaces they touch, leading to a growing interest in contactless payment options. With NFC, you don't need to hand over cash or cards to a cashier, which lowers the risk of spreading germs. As customers seek safer and cleaner ways to pay, the appeal of NFC technology keeps rising. It's comforting to know that you can complete a transaction without needing to make physical contact.

However, even with all the gains NFC has made in making payments easier and safer, worries about security are still a big deal. How can we be sure our sensitive information stays safe during these quick exchanges? The good news is that security is a top priority in NFC technology. The tokens created during transactions are time-sensitive and can only be used once. So, even if someone were to intercept a token, it wouldn't work for any future payments. Plus, NFC transactions use encryption protocols to protect the data as it moves, adding another layer of security.

On top of that, many mobile wallet apps use biometric authentication, like fingerprint or facial recognition, before allowing any payments. This provides an extra layer of protection, making sure that even if someone gets hold of your phone, they can't make payments without your permission. Imagine it as having a secret password known only to you before entering a secure vault. As technology keeps advancing, these security measures are likely to get even better, giving users greater peace of mind as they use digital payments.

Interestingly, NFC isn't just limited to contactless payments. This technology has a wide range of uses beyond shopping. From ticketing solutions for public transport to clever marketing strategies in stores, NFC can facilitate many different interactions. For example, picture walking into a museum and accessing in-depth information about an exhibit just by tapping your smartphone against a special NFC tag. This kind of technological integration into our everyday lives is becoming more common and opens up a world of possibilities that can enhance our experiences.

When we look at the world of payment technologies, it's helpful to compare NFC with other methods, such as QR codes. Both NFC and QR codes enable cashless transactions, but they work in very different ways. QR codes require users to scan a printed code using their devices, while NFC allows for instant data transfer just by being close. This basic difference affects not only user experience but also convenience. QR codes can work well, but they might need extra steps—like ensuring the code is visible and your camera is working properly. NFC, on the other hand, operates effortlessly with just a tap, offering users a smoother experience.

As technology continues to change, remembering that consumer education is key is essential. While NFC technology is gaining popularity, many people still don't know much about its benefits and capabilities. A well-informed consumer is more likely to adopt new payment methods and weave them into their daily routines. It's vital for businesses and financial institutions to provide clear instructions, tutorials, and information about NFC technology, helping to clarify the process and build trust with customers.

Looking ahead, the future of NFC technology is certainly exciting. The journey of digital payments is far from over, and NFC is set to play a crucial role in the next chapter. With ongoing innovations, we can expect improvements in security, faster transactions, and even greater convenience for users. As more businesses embrace contactless payment methods, we're likely to see a world where carrying cash or cards becomes a thing of the past, replaced by the easy, slick convenience of tapping our phones to complete transactions.

In this age of digital transformation, NFC technology offers more than just a way to pay. It represents a shift towards a future where our money interactions become smoother and more integrated into our daily lives. As we navigate this thrilling new landscape, it's vital to stay open to the opportunities that NFC technology brings, understanding that it's not just about the tech itself, but the experiences it creates for both consumers and businesses. The revolution is already underway, and NFC is leading the way into a cashless future, one tap at a time.

The Future of Wallets: Speculating on How Digital Wallets Might Evolve

As we find ourselves on the brink of a new financial era, it's fascinating to consider all the possibilities that could shape the future of digital wallets. Technology has evolved so quickly, turning ideas that once seemed far-off into our everyday lives, and digital wallets are a perfect example of this change. They have changed how we think about and handle money, pushing us to rethink what currency really means. With the rise of cryptocurrencies and improvements in security, we are starting to imagine a future where digital wallets become not just tools for making payments but also vital partners in our financial journeys.

  The boom in cryptocurrencies has been truly game-changing. Bitcoin, Ethereum, and many other digital coins have caught the attention of everyone from seasoned investors to the simply curious, reshaping our understanding of money. Digital wallets, which were initially made for storing traditional cash, are now evolving to support these new digital currencies. Picture an easy-to-use wallet app that doesn't just keep track of your dollars but also helps you manage and trade your cryptocurrency investments. You could check your balances, make trades, and get updates about market changes, all from one smooth interface. In this exciting future, digital wallets evolve into sophisticated financial centers, where both traditional and digital currencies work together, helping us navigate the shifting world of finance with confidence.

  As we think about this evolution, it's clear that we need to talk about security, too. Our wallets should not only be convenient but also safe. Imagine being able to pay for your morning coffee simply by glancing at your phone, which uses facial recognition to unlock your wallet, and your fingerprint to confirm the payment. This seamless process would make transactions quick while also giving us peace of mind in a world where data breaches and fraud are common. Biometric security is becoming more popular, and as technology continues to develop, we can look forward to even more innovations in this area. Picture a wallet that recognizes your unique heartbeat or listens to the patterns in your voice. These advancements would create a truly personal experience, ensuring that only you can access your funds while making payments as easy as breathing.

The idea of a cashless future brings with it significant social implications. For many, moving away from physical money could be a huge step toward greater financial inclusion. By breaking down the barriers that often limit access to banking services, people in underserved communities could gain financial tools that were previously out of reach. Digital wallets could act as gateways, opening up opportunities for savings accounts, loans, and investments. Imagine a young entrepreneur in a remote village being able to receive small loans directly through a digital wallet, helping to uplift their community and foster economic growth. This shift in finance could empower people to take charge of their financial futures, breaking free from cycles of poverty and encouraging entrepreneurship.

Yet, making the leap to a fully cashless society has its challenges. Relying solely on technology opens us up to various risks. What happens if there's a power outage or a natural disaster that knocks out internet access? A heavy reliance on digital wallets could leave some people in difficult situations, unable to complete financial transactions. It's important that we find a balance between embracing technological advancements and ensuring that we have backup plans for those rare but possible events. Building a strong infrastructure that can withstand crises will be key as we navigate this new frontier.

As digital wallets become more widespread, teaching users how to navigate these tools will also be crucial. Financial literacy needs to grow alongside these new technologies, giving individuals the skills they need to manage their finances confidently. Imagine programs that not only show people how to use a digital wallet but also how to budget, manage investments, and understand cryptocurrencies. These initiatives could empower individuals to make informed choices, creating a generation that is not only tech-savvy but also financially smart.

One of the most exciting possibilities for the future of digital wallets is the potential for them to merge with budgeting apps and investment platforms. Picture a central hub where you can see all your transactions in real-time, set budgeting goals, and receive alerts when you're getting close to your spending limits. Your wallet could analyze your spending patterns, suggest personalized budgeting options, and even recommend investment opportunities based on your goals. This comprehensive approach to personal finance would not only simplify money management but also promote healthier spending habits and long-term financial planning.

As we look ahead, flexibility will be critical in the face of rapid technological change. The digital wallet of the future needs to be adaptable, ready to incorporate new features and respond to emerging trends. Whether it's connecting with social media for peer-to-peer payments or using artificial intelligence to provide customized financial advice, the possibilities are endless. The key is to keep an open mind and be willing to embrace innovation while ensuring that user experience and security remain our top priorities.

Additionally, as digital wallets expand their capabilities, we can expect to see loyalty programs built right into these platforms. Imagine shopping for groceries and earning points that automatically apply to your favorite brands or local businesses. This would create a win-win situation: consumers would feel rewarded for their spending, while businesses could foster stronger connections with their customers. It's a great way to enrich the shopping experience and boost community engagement.

Of course, with every revolution come challenges. As digital wallets become commonplace, we must address concerns about privacy and data security. The more we use these platforms, the more valuable our personal information becomes, making it a tempting target for hackers. Finding the right balance between convenience and security is crucial. Regulatory frameworks may need to evolve to protect users, ensuring that companies prioritize privacy and data protection. In this new world, consumers will need to stay alert, advocating for transparency and accountability from the businesses handling their financial information.

Even amid all these changes, we need to keep our focus on the core values that have guided our financial systems for years: trust, transparency, and accessibility. These principles must be woven into the very fabric of our digital wallets, so as we move toward a cashless future, we do so with integrity. A digital wallet is more than just a tool; it represents our financial identities and the trust we place in the systems that manage our money.

As we imagine this future, let's remember that we are just at the beginning of this journey. The innovations we're seeing now are just a sneak peek of what's ahead. As technology continues to advance, we can expect digital wallets to evolve in ways we can't even foresee yet. The potential for connections with blockchain technology, artificial intelligence, and even the Internet of Things paints an exciting picture for what's to come.

To wrap it up, the future of digital wallets is filled with potential. They are on track to become essential parts of our financial lives, growing into comprehensive tools that not only make transactions easier but also promote financial literacy and inclusivity. The interaction between cryptocurrencies, biometric security, and user education will shape the world of digital finance, creating opportunities for individuals and communities to flourish.

While we welcome these advancements, we must also stay aware of the challenges this change brings. By focusing on education, security, and inclusivity, we can work toward a future where digital wallets enhance our financial interactions and contribute to a fairer and more empowered society. The revolution is already in motion, and as we press on, it's crucial to look ahead, ready to embrace the endless possibilities that await us.

Walter Bancroft

Chapter 5: Beyond Cards—Alternative Payment Methods

ACH and Wire Transfers: Exploring How Direct Bank Payments Operate

In an age where digital transactions are becoming the norm, the ways money transfers from one account to another are getting more attention. Traditional payment methods like cash and checks are gradually being replaced by electronic options that provide speed, convenience, and flexibility. Among these options, Automated Clearing House (ACH) transfers and wire transfers stand out as two key methods for making direct bank payments. Knowing how these alternatives work can really help you make better financial decisions and manage your money wisely.

Let's start with ACH transfers, which have become a vital part of our banking and payment systems. At its heart, ACH is a network that enables electronic payments and transfers between banks. It allows people and businesses to send money directly from one bank account to another without needing to use physical checks or cash. ACH transfers are incredibly useful; they are used for everything from payroll deposits to recurring bills, making them a go-to tool for many individuals and organizations alike.

ACH transactions work on a batch processing system. Instead of handling each transaction one by one—which could slow things down and increase costs—ACH transfers group several transactions together and process them all at once. This batching usually happens overnight, which allows for efficient fund movement while keeping costs down. For consumers, this means that although the transfer might not happen right away, the savings on transaction fees and the ease of setting up automated payments make ACH a great choice.

You may be wondering when you'd actually use ACH transfers in your daily life. They are especially popular for regular payments like rent, mortgage payments, and utility bills. Picture this: you have your monthly rent automatically taken out of your bank account. You can relax knowing your landlord will get the payment on time without you having to remember to write and mail a check every month. Likewise, many employers rely on ACH for payroll deposits, ensuring that workers receive their paychecks directly in their bank accounts when they should, which is a win-win for everyone involved.

While ACH transfers are widely used and usually budget-friendly, they do have some limitations. For example, they aren't the best option for urgent or same-day transactions. If you need to send money quickly—say, for an emergency repair or an unexpected bill—waiting for overnight processing just won't work. That's when wire transfers come into play, offering a solution for those urgent needs.

Wire transfers are another type of electronic fund transfer, but they work differently from ACH transactions. When you set up a wire transfer, the money moves directly from one bank to another in real-time. This speed is especially helpful for larger amounts of money or international transfers, where timing can be crucial. Unlike ACH, which processes transactions in batches, wire transfers are handled individually, allowing the recipient to access their funds immediately.

However, this speed often comes with a price. Wire transfers usually have higher fees compared to ACH transfers, which can make people hesitant to use them unless absolutely necessary. Plus, sending money internationally through wire transfers often involves navigating the SWIFT network, which can add some complications and delays in certain cases.

When it comes to their use, wire transfers are often preferred for significant financial transactions, like real estate purchases, business deals, or urgent personal transfers. For example, if you're buying a house and need to send a large deposit to secure the property, a wire transfer provides the quick and reliable option you need to complete that deal without delay.

When we compare these two methods of direct bank payment, it becomes clear that each has its advantages and disadvantages. On one side, ACH transfers are cost-effective, widely used for everyday transactions, and perfect for those looking to automate their payments. On the other hand, wire transfers excel in speed and urgency, making them essential for large transactions or situations where time is of the essence.

For those looking to manage their finances wisely, knowing when to use ACH versus wire transfers can greatly influence budgeting and cash flow. For routine expenses and regular payments, ACH transfers can save you both time and money, allowing you to set it up and forget it until the next bill comes. On the flip side, for immediate needs—especially involving larger amounts or international transfers—wire transfers can be a lifesaver, ensuring that funds are delivered right when you need them.

As we look deeper into the world of alternative payment methods, the differences between ACH and wire transfers highlight the growing complexity of our financial landscape. Understanding these options empowers us to make informed choices, ensuring that our hard-earned money moves effectively and securely according to our needs. With a better grasp of these two direct bank payment methods, we can tailor our financial strategies to save money and improve our overall financial management.

By breaking down how ACH and wire transfers work, we help readers navigate their financial lives with more confidence. Each transaction contributes to the larger story of personal finance, and knowing when to use these tools is crucial for creating a balanced approach to managing money. As we continue exploring alternative payment methods, we can expect the landscape to become richer and more varied, offering even more ways for consumers to connect with their finances in creative ways.

Online Payment Platforms: Investigating PayPal, Venmo, and Their Convenience

The way we manage our money has changed dramatically in the digital age, making transactions quicker and easier than ever before. Among the many innovations we've seen, online payment platforms have truly reshaped how we handle our finances day-to-day. Whether you're splitting a dinner bill with friends, paying for a service, or shopping online, these platforms allow us to make payments with just a few clicks. Two of the biggest names in this arena are PayPal and Venmo, both of which have carved out unique roles and changed how we think about exchanging money in our increasingly cashless world.

Let's start with PayPal, a name that's almost become a household word when it comes to online payments. Founded in the late 1990s, PayPal has established itself as a key player in e-commerce, letting users send and receive payments securely while offering important buyer protections. Its global reach and flexibility make it attractive to both consumers and businesses, enabling transactions across different currencies and borders.

At its heart, PayPal works by linking your bank account or credit card to your PayPal account. This connection makes it easy to transfer money without needing cash or checks. Think about how convenient it is to shop online—rather than searching for your credit card in your wallet, you can simply log into your PayPal account, click a few buttons, and complete your purchase in just seconds. For frequent shoppers, especially on sites like eBay, PayPal allows you to manage multiple transactions without the hassle of re-entering your card details each time.

One of the standout features for many online shoppers is PayPal's buyer protection. If you buy something that doesn't arrive or isn't what you expected, PayPal gives you a safety net. You can dispute the transaction and possibly get your money back. This sense of security has built trust among consumers, encouraging more people to shop online.

However, it's good to remember that while PayPal is a powerful tool, it does come with fees. For merchants, these transaction costs can add up, leading some to look for other options.

Now, let's talk about Venmo, a platform that has become incredibly popular, especially among younger users. Although it's owned by PayPal, Venmo stands out because of its focus on social connections. The app is designed for easy peer-to-peer payments, making it perfect for casual transactions between friends and family.

Imagine you're out at a restaurant with friends, and the bill arrives. Instead of fumbling around with cash or writing a check, you can quickly pull up the Venmo app, enter the amount, and send money to the friend who paid for the meal. The process is fast and friendly; Venmo even includes a "social feed" where you can see payments made by friends, complete with fun emojis and notes. This social aspect turns what used to be a mundane task into something more engaging and enjoyable.

That said, it's important to pay attention to Venmo's privacy settings. By default, your transactions are public, which means anyone can see your payment history unless you change this setting. Many users may unknowingly share too much information, which can lead to awkward situations. So, just like with any online platform, it's essential to understand privacy settings in order to keep your personal information safe.

Both PayPal and Venmo prioritize security, which is crucial in our digital world. They use encryption, two-factor authentication, and fraud detection systems to keep users safe while navigating online payments. However, even the best security can't completely eliminate risks. For instance, while PayPal offers strong buyer protection, scams can still happen, especially in peer-to-peer transactions. Users should stay alert and cautious, particularly when dealing with unfamiliar individuals.

When using these platforms, it's also good to keep an eye on the fees. PayPal charges fees for instant transfers and for receiving payments in business transactions, while Venmo may charge when you choose an instant transfer instead of waiting for a standard transfer, which can take one to three business days. If you're careful about your spending, knowing these costs is essential for keeping your budget on track.

As we explore online payments, understanding how these platforms fit into the financial landscape is key. They are more than just payment tools; they reflect a shift in how we think about money. The ease of sending money with just a tap has made us more spontaneous in our spending. It's now common to send a few dollars to a friend for coffee, something that might have seemed too trivial in the past.

However, this ease of use has its downsides. The simplicity of these platforms can sometimes lead to overspending, and it's easy to lose sight of your overall financial situation. When payments are just a click away, being aware of your spending becomes even more important. Developing good budgeting habits is essential as we navigate the world of digital payments.

Also, as these platforms grow, they continuously introduce new features to improve user experience. For example, PayPal has started offering options for cryptocurrency, allowing users to buy, hold, and sell digital currencies like Bitcoin right from their accounts. Similarly, Venmo now lets users buy and sell stocks through the app. These developments show how these platforms are trying to keep up with what consumers want and how the financial landscape is changing, reinforcing their importance in the world of online payments.

The influence of online payment platforms extends beyond convenience; they've really changed how we perceive and handle money. Where cash once dominated, a large number of transactions now take place in the digital space. As more people trust these platforms, they give users a way to engage with their finances in a more immediate and dynamic manner.

To wrap it all up, both PayPal and Venmo represent a clear shift towards digital payments, offering innovative solutions to meet various needs and preferences. While PayPal is a strong choice for buyers and sellers in the e-commerce world, Venmo's social features make it a hit for casual transactions among friends. Each platform has its own unique perks and downsides, so it's vital for users to consider their individual habits and requirements before diving in.

With these platforms at our fingertips, we have unprecedented access to financial tools that can significantly streamline our everyday transactions. As we continue to explore the changing landscape of payment methods, grasping how to navigate these online payment platforms is becoming increasingly vital for achieving financial success. By using these tools wisely, consumers can improve their budgeting strategies, simplify their spending, and take charge of their financial futures. In this new age of digital finance, knowledge truly is power, and the more informed we are, the better we can navigate the complexities of our financial lives.

The Rise of Buy Now, Pay Later: Examining New Financing Options at Checkout

In recent years, a new financial trend has caught the eye of both shoppers and retailers: Buy Now, Pay Later (BNPL). This fresh payment model provides a way for consumers to buy what they want without the pressure of paying the full amount upfront. Instead of shelling out the total price all at once, BNPL lets you break down that cost into smaller, often interest-free payments spread over weeks or months. This change in how we think about payment has struck a chord with younger shoppers who are figuring out their financial independence. They are looking for options that fit with their spending habits and lifestyles.

The way BNPL works is pretty simple, and it fits nicely into the checkout process. Picture this: you're browsing online for a new pair of shoes. After picking your size and color, you head to checkout and see a variety of payment options. Among these, the attractive BNPL choice stands out, letting you pay just a fraction of the total today, with the rest due later. This option taps into our desire for instant gratification while still giving us a sense of control over our finances.

Typically, when you choose BNPL, you can pick a payment plan that suits you best. You might decide to pay a quarter of the price now and spread the rest out into equal payments due every two weeks. This setup allows you to enjoy your new shoes while managing your cash flow. Big-name retailers, from fashion brands to electronics stores, have jumped on the BNPL bandwagon to make shopping easier and give consumers a chance to buy items they might have thought twice about.

But the appeal of BNPL goes beyond just convenience; it connects to a mindset where we buy first and think later. This way of thinking is especially strong among younger generations, who are used to getting what they want quickly. The chance to get an item without feeling the financial pinch right away can be hard to resist. It's like being able to have your cake and eat it too, with the promise of easy payments right there at checkout.

While BNPL has its perks, it also comes with some important things to think about. As more people choose this payment option, it's vital to consider how it changes our spending habits. The freedom to buy now and pay later can lead to impulsive buys that might not fit into a reasonable budget. When the payment isn't due immediately, it's easy to forget about the long-term effects of those spending choices. This can create a cycle of overspending, where the excitement of new purchases overshadows the need for careful financial planning.

For some folks, BNPL can lead to an unhealthy relationship with money. The ease of making payments can mask the reality of accumulating debt. As those monthly payments pile up, it's all too easy to lose track of what you owe. The real cost of your purchases can start to blur, leading you to feel more secure about your finances than you actually are. A recent study found that many BNPL users struggled to keep up with payment schedules, raising valid concerns about the wider effects of this payment method.

That said, it's crucial to understand budgeting now more than ever, especially with BNPL options readily available. By developing strong financial habits, consumers can enjoy the benefits of flexible payment plans while also reducing the risks of overspending. Creating a budget that covers both immediate needs and future payments can empower shoppers to make smart choices and keep their financial health in check.

Given these challenges, it's important for consumers to adopt strategies that encourage smart financial habits. One good step is setting a monthly spending limit for BNPL purchases that reflects your actual financial situation. By deciding how much you can spend each month, you can keep a tight grip on your spending. Additionally, focusing on needs versus wants can help prioritize important purchases over impulse buys.

Being clear on the terms and conditions linked to BNPL agreements is also vital. While many BNPL plans promote interest-free installments, hidden fees or penalties for late payments can quickly turn a great deal into a financial headache. Reading the fine print is essential to avoid surprises later on. Take the time to understand the terms and the potential outcomes of missing payments, like extra fees and detrimental impacts on your credit score.

It's also important to consider both the risks and the rewards that come with BNPL. The chance to shop without immediate financial stress is appealing, but this convenience can lead to some serious pitfalls. As more consumers choose BNPL, they need to stay alert to the possible downsides that come with it. Accumulating debt can be a slippery slope, especially for younger people who might not have the experience to navigate tricky financial waters.

One major risk with BNPL is how it can affect credit scores. Many BNPL companies report payment histories to credit bureaus, meaning missed or late payments can stick with you for a long time. Therefore, careless use of BNPL can hurt your creditworthiness, making it tougher to get loans or credit down the line. Users need to keep a close eye on their payment schedules to ensure they meet their commitments and maintain a healthy credit score.

Furthermore, the psychological effects of using BNPL can create a disconnect from the true costs of buying things. When payments are put off, people might underestimate how much they are actually spending. This can lead to a dangerous cycle of debt that only becomes clear when it's too late. Regularly checking your financial situation and keeping track of what you owe is key to staying within your means.

On the brighter side, BNPL offers real benefits, such as making products more accessible. For many shoppers, the ability to buy bigger-ticket items without feeling immediate financial pressure opens doors that would otherwise remain closed. This can be especially helpful for those just starting out in their financial journey or for those who might struggle to qualify for traditional credit. BNPL acts as a bridge, allowing consumers to interact with the market in ways that fit their financial realities.

Moreover, when used responsibly, BNPL can actually encourage healthier spending habits. Breaking down larger purchases into smaller installments may keep people from relying on high-interest credit cards or loans. This feature can promote a more thoughtful approach to spending, pushing individuals to think carefully about their purchases and focus on what's truly important.

In summary, the rise of Buy Now, Pay Later reflects a change in how consumers prefer flexible ways to pay. As society evolves, so does our approach to managing money. However, this comes with a call for responsibility. While BNPL has its attractive perks, it's vital for consumers to tread carefully, staying informed about their financial choices.

Ultimately, the aim is to find a balance between enjoying the ease of instant purchases and keeping a stable financial footing. By grasping how BNPL works, understanding its effects on behavior, and weighing the pros and cons, individuals can make smart decisions that fit their unique financial situations.

As we welcome the ease of modern payment methods, it's crucial to remember that true value in a purchase isn't just about acquiring it but also managing its cost wisely. In a world full of tempting offers and appealing payment plans, staying connected to your financial reality will guide you toward smarter spending and a brighter financial future. The rise of Buy Now, Pay Later is more than just a trend; it symbolizes a broader shift in how we handle financial transactions and serves as a reminder of the importance of financial literacy in navigating today's consumer landscape.

Chapter 6: Cryptocurrencies—The New Frontier

Blockchain Basics: Breaking Down the Technology Behind Bitcoin and Ethereum

The world of cryptocurrencies can feel like a dazzling magic show, with coins appearing and disappearing, leaving many of us scratching our heads. But behind this spectacle is an incredible technology called blockchain. This technology not only supports cryptocurrencies like Bitcoin and Ethereum but also represents a major shift in how we think about transactions and trust in our digital lives. Getting to know blockchain is like opening a door to a whole new world of possibilities in finance.

In simple terms, blockchain is a decentralized digital ledger that securely keeps track of transactions across a network of computers. Imagine a shared notebook among friends. Each page of this notebook is a block that lists all the transactions made between them. Once a page is full, it can't be changed, and the notebook grows as more pages are added, creating a chain of trust. This shared system of record-keeping means everyone can see the same information, and most importantly, this information can't be changed.

Let's break it down a bit more. Each block in the blockchain has three key parts. First, there's the transaction data, which shows who sent what to whom. Next, there's a unique hash, like a digital fingerprint, that identifies that block and its contents. Finally, each block also includes the hash of the previous block, linking them in a time sequence. This clever linking not only keeps the order of transactions but also boosts security. If someone tried to change the information in a block, it would alter that block's hash, breaking the connection to the next block.

Now, let's talk about nodes. These are the individual computers that make up the blockchain network. Think of nodes as the watchful guardians of the communal notebook. They check transactions and keep copies of the ledger. If you were to look at a blockchain network, you'd see many nodes all holding the same notebook, ensuring everyone has the same information.

These nodes play a vital role in keeping the system secure and trustworthy. Among them are miners, especially in the case of Bitcoin. These miners take on the added job of solving tough math problems to validate transactions and create new blocks. For their hard work, miners earn cryptocurrency rewards. This process of mining not only produces new coins but also adds blocks to the chain, making the network even more secure.

What's truly remarkable about blockchain is its built-in transparency and security features. At its heart is a consensus mechanism, like Proof of Work, which makes sure everyone in the network agrees on what the ledger says. This decentralized agreement helps build trust in a system where users don't have to depend on a central authority. Picture if each friend in the group had their own copy of the shared notebook; if one person tried to cheat and change a transaction, the others could easily spot the mistake and reject the altered entry.

Another amazing aspect of blockchain is smart contracts, which change the way agreements are made and carried out. Smart contracts are self-executing agreements with the terms written directly into code. They operate on platforms like Ethereum, allowing automatic execution of transactions when certain conditions are met. Imagine setting up a smart contract for a birthday party; when the big day arrives, the agreement automatically sends out invitations and confirms the venue, all without needing a middleman. This innovative feature of blockchain opens up new possibilities, extending its uses beyond just handling money.

Transparency is a key characteristic of blockchain technology. Every transaction is recorded in real-time and can be viewed by anyone who has access to the blockchain, creating an open environment where accountability can flourish. This is especially useful in industries like supply chain management, where tracking products and verifying their authenticity is crucial. By using blockchain, businesses can make sure every step of a product's journey is recorded, building trust between consumers and producers.

While blockchain technology is praised for its strengths, it does face some challenges. Scalability is a big concern; as more transactions happen, the need for processing power and storage increases. Additionally, the energy use of mining operations, particularly those that use Proof of Work, has come under fire due to their impact on the environment. Finding sustainable ways to tackle these challenges will be essential as blockchain technology aims for wider use.

As we dive deeper into the world of cryptocurrencies, it becomes clear that blockchain is not just a technical curiosity; it's a foundational innovation that could change our financial systems for good. Understanding how it works is key for anyone looking to navigate the evolving landscape of digital currencies. The heart of blockchain technology is its ability to create trust without needing middlemen, allowing people to take charge of their transactions and financial dealings.

With this solid understanding of blockchain technology, we're ready to explore how cryptocurrencies work within this framework. We'll compare them to traditional payment systems and weigh the benefits and challenges they offer to both consumers and businesses. As we journey into the world of digital currencies, remember that we're not just witnessing the rise of Bitcoin and Ethereum; we're experiencing the beginning of a whole new financial era.

Crypto Transactions

The way we handle money is changing, and with the growth of cryptocurrencies, we're seeing a shift that shakes up how we usually make payments. Picture a world where sending money is as fast as sending a text message, where no middleman is needed, and where your security and privacy are greatly improved. This is what cryptocurrencies offer, standing in sharp contrast to the traditional systems that have managed our financial dealings for so long.

Let's take a moment to think about the traditional banking system. Most of us know how it works. When you want to send money to a friend—maybe to split the bill for dinner or chip in for a group gift—you usually grab your banking app or go online. You enter your friend's information, put in the amount, and hit send. But here's the catch: the money doesn't just zoom off instantly. Instead, your request goes through a maze of middlemen, including your bank and possibly your friend's bank, along with any payment processors involved. Depending on the banks, the time of day, and the type of transaction, this can take anywhere from a few hours to several days to finish.

Now, let's compare that to a cryptocurrency transaction. Imagine you want to send Bitcoin to a friend. All you need is their wallet address—kind of like their digital ID. After entering the amount and double-checking the details, you hit send. In just a few minutes, or sometimes even seconds, the transaction is logged on the blockchain, and your friend sees the money in their wallet. The contrast is clear; what used to take days now happens almost instantly.

One of the biggest perks of cryptocurrency transactions is speed. In a world that craves efficiency, this quickness is a game-changer. While traditional banks have to work around business hours, regulations, and the complexities of international transfers, cryptocurrencies break free from these limitations. You can start and finish a transaction at any hour, day or night, with hardly any wait. This not only fits our fast-moving lives but also opens up new opportunities for businesses that operate across different time zones.

Looking deeper into the differences, security stands out as another key point.

Traditional banks, even with their strong systems, aren't immune to issues. Data breaches, identity theft, and fraud are problems that these institutions often face, leading to big financial losses for both banks and customers. Cryptocurrencies, on the other hand, use advanced cryptographic methods to keep transactions secure. Each transaction is encrypted and linked to past transactions through complex algorithms, creating a strong security network. If someone tries to tamper with the transaction history, they would have to change every block in the chain, which is incredibly hard to do because of the decentralized nature of blockchain technology.

However, it's important to remember that no system is perfect. While cryptocurrencies can offer better security against certain types of fraud, they also come with their own risks. The anonymity that cryptocurrencies provide can be a double-edged sword. While it keeps users' personal information safe from prying eyes, it can also lead to misuse, like money laundering or financing illegal activities. The challenge is finding a balance between protecting privacy and ensuring accountability.

Cost is another vital factor in this discussion. Traditional banks often charge steep fees for international money transfers, conversion rates, and service charges, which can add up quickly, especially for those who send money often. For example, if you wanted to transfer funds overseas, you might end up paying fees that take a big chunk out of the money you're sending. On the flip side, cryptocurrency transactions usually have lower fees, especially for cross-border transfers. While fees can vary based on network traffic and transaction size, many users discover that cryptocurrencies offer a more cost-effective way to send money internationally.

Imagine a family wanting to send money from the U.S. to relatives in Mexico. Using a traditional remittance service might mean paying a fee that could be as high as 10% of the amount sent, not to mention poor exchange rates. In contrast, sending the same amount in Bitcoin might only cost a few dollars, allowing more of the money to actually reach the family member who needs it.

Moreover, our understanding of privacy has changed. With traditional payment methods, personal information is often shared with multiple parties, like banks and payment processors. This sharing can raise real concerns about data privacy and security. In contrast, cryptocurrency transactions offer a level of anonymity. While every transaction is recorded on the blockchain, the identities of the people involved don't have to be shared. Instead, users are represented by unique wallet addresses. This kind of privacy can be appealing, particularly in a time when data breaches are so common.

However, it's crucial to note that this anonymity can also lead to shady practices, creating challenges for regulators who are trying to promote transparency.

To really grasp how cryptocurrency transactions work, it's important to understand the practical steps involved in making a crypto transfer. The first step is setting up a digital wallet, a secure app or device where users keep their cryptocurrencies. There are two main types of wallets: hot wallets, which are connected to the internet and convenient for regular transactions, and cold wallets, which are offline and provide extra security for long-term storage. Picking the right wallet depends on what you need and how often you plan to use it.

Once you have your wallet set up, the next step is to fund it by buying cryptocurrency from an exchange. This usually means linking a bank account or using another form of payment to get your digital coins. After that, making a transaction is pretty straightforward: you enter the recipient's wallet address, type in the amount, and confirm the transfer. This simplicity is one of the most attractive aspects of cryptocurrencies.

That said, security should always be a top priority. It's wise to take steps to protect yourself, like turning on two-factor authentication for your accounts and regularly backing up your wallet information. Users also need to be on the lookout for phishing scams and fraud, as the decentralized nature of cryptocurrencies means that once a transaction is confirmed, it can't be undone. Unlike traditional banks, which offer some protection for unauthorized transactions, cryptocurrencies don't provide that safety net, making it crucial for users to keep their assets secure.

As we explore this exciting new world of digital currency, it's essential to recognize that while cryptocurrencies present benefits like faster transactions, better security, and lower costs, they also come with risks and challenges. The conversation around privacy and accountability is likely to continue as more people and businesses consider these alternative payment methods.

In the end, the rise of cryptocurrencies calls for a rethinking of how we handle transactions in our daily lives, blurring the lines between traditional banking and the innovative opportunities that blockchain technology brings. As digital currencies continue to gain popularity, understanding the details of how their transactions work will help individuals make informed choices in this rapidly changing financial landscape, challenging the norms of our financial systems and paving the way for a new era of cashless commerce.

Challenges and Opportunities: Discussing the Hurdles of Mainstream Crypto Adoption

The world of cryptocurrencies can feel like the Wild West of finance. It's a thrilling yet chaotic space, full of promise and risk. As digital currencies begin to find their footing in the global scene, we need to carefully navigate the tough challenges and exciting opportunities that lie ahead. Cryptocurrencies have the power to change financial systems, but their journey toward widespread acceptance is filled with obstacles like confusing regulations, unpredictable markets, and a general lack of public knowledge.

To really understand what's going on, let's look at the regulatory challenges cryptocurrencies face. There's no single set of rules governing cryptocurrencies worldwide, leading to a confusing mix of regulations that differ dramatically from one country to another. Some nations welcome cryptocurrencies, viewing them as a chance for innovation and growth, while others react with skepticism, even banning them due to fears about how they might disrupt traditional financial systems. For example, China has taken a tough approach, cracking down on cryptocurrency trading and initial coin offerings (ICOs) because they worry about losing control over financial markets. On the other hand, countries like El Salvador have made headlines by accepting Bitcoin as legal tender, highlighting the stark differences in how governments view digital currencies.

For businesses wanting to use cryptocurrencies, this regulatory maze can be tough to navigate. Imagine trying to create something new while constantly dodging hurdles and red tape. Companies must keep up with the ever-changing rules to avoid costly mistakes. When regulations are inconsistent, it can hold back innovation. Startups might hesitate to invest in new ideas when the rules can change at any moment. This uncertainty can stifle the growth of the crypto industry, making it hard for it to establish itself as a legitimate player in the global economy.

Another major issue is the wild price swings often seen in cryptocurrencies. Their values can change dramatically, like a rollercoaster ride, going up one day and crashing down the next. For instance, Bitcoin might hit a record high one week only to take a nosedive the next, leaving investors confused and worried about their losses. This kind of volatility raises real questions for anyone thinking of using or investing in cryptocurrencies. How can you trust a currency that might lose half its value overnight? For many, the risks of investing in cryptocurrencies feel too great compared to the potential rewards. Businesses that accept cryptocurrencies face similar concerns; these fluctuating values can eat into profits and make it tricky to manage cash flow.

Additionally, many people are hesitant to embrace cryptocurrency due to a lack of understanding. The technical jargon and complex ideas associated with blockchain and cryptocurrencies can be overwhelming for the average person. Even professionals like healthcare workers, teachers, and engineers might find themselves lost when faced with terms like hash rates, private keys, and smart contracts. This knowledge gap can slow down the acceptance of cryptocurrencies. Until more people are comfortable with the underlying technology, it seems that widespread adoption will be a challenge. We need to simplify cryptocurrencies and equip the public with the knowledge necessary to navigate this new financial world.

When it comes to security, cryptocurrencies have unique perks but also significant risks. While the technology behind cryptocurrencies is designed to secure transactions and protect user identities, vulnerabilities still exist. Notable hacking incidents, like the infamous Mt. Gox hack where hundreds of millions worth of Bitcoin was stolen, have left users feeling uneasy. Plus, because cryptocurrencies operate in a relatively unregulated space, there's often little recourse for users who fall victim to theft or fraud. The decentralized nature of blockchain means transactions can't be reversed, which, while secure, can leave victims without any safety net.

Despite these challenges, the opportunities that come with cryptocurrencies are truly groundbreaking. One of the biggest advantages is the potential for financial inclusion. Billions of people around the world don't have access to traditional banking services. Cryptocurrencies could offer these individuals a way to join the global economy. In areas where banks are scarce or non-existent, a smartphone and an internet connection can be a gateway to digital currencies. This shift in finance could empower marginalized communities, allowing them to engage in commerce, save, and invest without the hurdles set by conventional banking systems.

Additionally, lower transaction fees present an exciting opportunity. For both businesses and individuals, the ability to send money across borders without hefty fees can be a game changer. Traditional remittance services often charge high rates, taking away a chunk of the money being sent. Cryptocurrencies can significantly reduce these costs, ensuring more of the funds actually make it to their intended recipients. For example, imagine a worker in the United States sending money back home to family in a developing country, only to see a large portion vanish into fees. With cryptocurrencies, this worker can send the same amount with little to no fees, significantly benefiting their loved ones.

The innovations spurred by cryptocurrencies stretch beyond just making transactions easier. They also offer fresh ways to think about value and ownership. The rise of decentralized finance (DeFi) has allowed users to lend, borrow, and trade without needing intermediaries. By cutting out middlemen, users can enjoy lower fees and greater control over their financial transactions. Plus, the emergence of non-fungible tokens (NFTs) has changed how we view ownership of digital assets. Artists, musicians, and content creators can now monetize their work in groundbreaking ways, directly connecting with their audience and maintaining more control over their intellectual property.

In this mix of challenges and opportunities, it's vital to keep a balanced view. The path to mainstream crypto adoption will certainly have its ups and downs. Yet, these challenges can also open doors to innovation and transformation in the financial world. As regulations become clearer, market volatility stabilizes, public knowledge increases, and security measures improve, the chance for cryptocurrencies to revolutionize how we handle transactions becomes more real.

Looking ahead, we should recognize that the future of cryptocurrencies won't be straightforward. It will require teamwork among governments, businesses, and users to create a balanced environment where innovation can flourish while still providing safety against risks. Teaching the public about the benefits and downsides of cryptocurrencies will be key to building trust and encouraging adoption. The dream of a decentralized financial system that offers equal access to economic opportunities is within reach, but it will take a united effort from everyone involved to tackle the complexities ahead.

As we stand on the edge of this financial revolution, it's important to be both careful and hopeful. The challenges may seem overwhelming, but every major transformation in history has faced its own set of hurdles. The possibilities for financial inclusion, lower transaction costs, and innovative ideas are enticing. By confronting these obstacles directly and recognizing the potential, we can embrace the exciting world of cryptocurrencies and move toward a future where finance is more accessible, efficient, and responsive to everyone's needs.

Chapter 7: Securing the Transaction—Fraud and Protection

The Digital Fraud Landscape

As we step into a new era of financial transactions, the familiar sounds of cash jingling in our pockets are being replaced by the soft beeps of smartphones and the swipe of credit cards. We're finding ourselves in an expansive digital world. This new age of payment systems offers incredible conveniences, allowing us to buy everything from our morning coffee to a luxurious vacation with just a few taps. However, with every new technology, there's a shadowy side that targets the unaware and the uninformed. While we enjoy the perks of digital innovation, it's vital to highlight the many types of fraud that hide beneath the surface of seemingly harmless transactions.

One of the most frequent scams we encounter in our connected world is phishing. This doesn't involve fishing rods and lakes; rather, it's about scammers casting a wide net online, hoping to catch unsuspecting victims. Phishing scams usually appear as emails or messages from companies we trust, like banks or well-known online stores. These messages often use urgent language designed to provoke fear or anxiety, tricking you into providing personal information such as passwords or Social Security numbers. The cleverness of these scams has increased significantly, making them harder to spot.

Picture this: you receive an email that looks just like one from your bank, complete with its logo and branding. The message claims there's suspicious activity on your account, urging you to click a link and verify your details to prevent being locked out. You click quickly, driven by fear of theft, only to discover you've handed your sensitive information to a scammer. Sadly, this scenario plays out daily in homes around the world, and as long as the internet connects us, phishers will continually invent new ways to exploit our worries and trust.

Identity theft is another frightening part of the digital fraud scene. It's like having your home broken into while you're away, leaving you with a chilling reminder of the invasion. Dishonest people can gather enough personal information about someone to impersonate them, opening credit accounts, taking out loans, and making big purchases in their name—often without any immediate indication that something is wrong. The impact of identity theft can be devastating, causing ruined credit scores and long investigations that drain both time and emotional energy. It serves as a harsh reminder that while our digital lives offer convenience, they also expose us to those who want to misuse our identities for financial gain.

Transaction fraud adds yet another layer of complexity to the digital payment world. In this case, criminals skip the need for personal information by directly attacking the transaction itself. This can lead to unauthorized charges on a credit card or the use of stolen payment details to make purchases. With the growth of online shopping, it's easier than ever for a fraudster to target unsuspecting customers. Imagine yourself enjoying a late-night shopping spree online. You find a stunning designer handbag at an unbeatable price from a site you've never heard of, and with just a few clicks, you complete the purchase. It's only later that you realize that the handbag was just a bait-and-switch, and now a scammer has disappeared with your money.

However, the fraud landscape isn't just about the tactics used by criminals. It also involves the ever-evolving technologies designed to protect us from these threats. Enter encryption and tokenization, two reliable defenders looking out for our digital transactions. Encryption works like a secret code, scrambling data so that only the person it's meant for can read it. Tokenization replaces sensitive information with unique identification symbols, or tokens, which have no value outside of a specific transaction. Together, these technologies work tirelessly behind the scenes to keep our personal and financial information safe as it travels through the vast digital space.

It's not just the companies and service providers that have the duty to protect our transactions. As consumers, we play a crucial role in this security story. By staying informed and adopting smart habits, we can lower our risk of falling victim to fraud. Simple actions like regularly checking our bank statements, using strong and unique passwords, and being cautious of unsolicited messages can build a strong defense against would-be criminals. Recognizing the warning signs of potential scams can empower us to act quickly when something seems off.

As we navigate this complex world of digital payments, we find ourselves at a crossroads: do we let the fear of fraud freeze us in place, or do we equip ourselves with knowledge and awareness, becoming savvy consumers? The choice is ours, and the route we take will shape not just our security level but also our overall confidence in the digital transactions that have become part of our everyday lives. The real challenge is not just to see the risks but also to understand the steps we can take to protect ourselves, ensuring that our journey into cashless payments is not tainted by the threat of fraud. As we dive deeper into how to secure our transactions, the goal is not just to recognize the dangers but to empower ourselves with the tools and knowledge needed to thrive in this digital age with confidence.

Encryption and Tokenization: Understanding How Your Data is Kept Safe

In a world where digital transactions are part of our daily lives, it's important to take a closer look at the technology that works hard to keep our financial data safe. Picture a lively marketplace buzzing with vendors, each trying to attract eager buyers showcasing their best goods. In this vibrant setting, your data—your sensitive financial information—makes its way between merchants and consumers, just like shoppers moving between stalls. But what if, in all that excitement, someone were to snatch your purse or sneak a peek at your receipts? This is where strong methods like encryption and tokenization come into play, acting like the vigilant guardians of our digital marketplace.

Encryption is all about turning data into a code that's unreadable to anyone who doesn't have the right access. Think of it as a secret language shared only between you and your trusted friends. When you send a message, your words get scrambled, and only the person with the right key can understand it. For example, when you make an online purchase, your credit card information and personal details are encrypted before they even leave your device. This means that even if a cybercriminal tries to grab your data while it's moving through the internet, all they'll see is a confusing jumble of letters and numbers, completely useless to them.

A key player in this process is the Secure Socket Layer (SSL) certificate. You've probably noticed that little padlock icon in your web browser's address bar. That's SSL at work, creating a secure, encrypted connection between your web server and your browser. When you visit a site that uses SSL, your data is protected through encryption, which helps keep it safe from prying eyes. This is especially crucial when you're entering sensitive information, like your credit card details or personal information. If you think of the Internet as a busy highway, SSL acts like a guardrail, keeping your car from veering off into dangerous territory.

You might be curious how encryption fits into the bigger picture of online transactions. Every time you make a purchase online, your details go through this encryption process. Your credit card information is changed into a secure code that can only be read with the right key. This not only keeps your data safe but also builds trust between you and the merchant. In a world where trust matters so much, knowing that your information is being carefully handled makes it easier to click "Buy Now" without second-guessing.

While encryption provides strong protection, tokenization adds another layer of security for our information. Think of tokenization as swapping out your real valuables for tokens—these tokens have no value outside their specific use. In payment processing, tokenization replaces sensitive data, like your credit card number, with unique symbols that keep the important parts of the data while hiding the sensitive stuff. For example, when you make a purchase, your actual credit card number might be replaced with a token, like a random mix of letters and numbers that only makes sense to the server handling the transaction.

This method doesn't just boost security; it also reduces the risks of storing sensitive data. If hackers were to get into a merchant's database, they wouldn't find anything useful. Instead of actual credit card numbers, they'd only find tokens—meaningless outside their intended transactions. Tokenization has truly changed the game for financial services, significantly lowering the chances of sensitive data falling into the wrong hands. It's like having a vault where only certain keys can unlock the valuable treasures inside; without those keys, everything remains safe and sound.

In practice, you'll find tokenization being widely used in mobile payment systems and digital wallets. When you save your credit card information in a mobile app, the app creates a token to store instead of your real card number. So, if someone ever gets access to your mobile wallet, they'll just see a bunch of tokens instead of the keys to your financial kingdom. Moreover, using tokenization in payment systems allows for smooth transactions while keeping security tight, which is a win-win for both customers and businesses.

Now, let's take a closer look at secure payment gateways—the unsung heroes of online transactions. A payment gateway works like a digital broker for transactions, taking your payment information, securely sending it, and returning the confirmation you need. It acts as a middleman between you and the merchant, making sure your sensitive details are exchanged safely without the risk of being exposed.

Popular third-party services like PayPal and Stripe have completely changed how we think about online transactions. When you use these services, you're trusting them with your payment information while shopping on different websites. The great thing about this setup is the extra security layer; your credit card data is never directly shared with the merchant. Instead, these payment gateways handle all your sensitive information, encrypting and tokenizing it behind the scenes to keep it safe from potential threats.

Let's imagine a fun scenario: you're on a late-night online shopping spree, browsing through a website that has everything you could want, from stylish clothes to the latest tech gadgets. When you decide to buy a new pair of sneakers, the site asks for your credit card details. Here's where the magic happens: before your information ever reaches the merchant, it gets sent through a secure payment gateway. Your details are encrypted into an unreadable format, and a token is created in its place. The merchant receives this token instead of your actual card details, ensuring they never see your sensitive financial information.

This whole process protects your data during the transaction and allows you to feel more relaxed while shopping. Knowing that your payment information is shielded by strong measures like encryption and tokenization gives you the confidence to browse the digital marketplace without worry. The added privacy and security from these technologies help you explore the wide range of products and services online without the fear of falling victim to fraud.

While technology plays a big role in protecting our digital transactions, it's also important to remember that our awareness and habits matter just as much. As consumers, understanding how encryption and tokenization work gives us a sense of control over the cashless world. By adopting habits that put our security first, like using strong passwords and regularly checking our financial accounts, we can strengthen the efforts of the technologies meant to protect us.

Also, staying aware of potential scams and fraud tactics helps us spot warning signs and take action. Just like you wouldn't stroll through a dark alley without being cautious, you shouldn't navigate the online world without keeping an eye out for dangers.

As we learn more about how our transactions work, we can explore digital payments with confidence. The combination of encryption, tokenization, and secure payment gateways is a strong team dedicated to keeping our data safe.

On this journey toward understanding the financial system, recognizing the importance of these protective technologies can change how we interact with digital transactions. Instead of viewing these advancements with suspicion, we can embrace them, knowing they work to protect our interests.

So, the next time you're about to make an online purchase, remember the invisible shields of encryption and tokenization standing guard over your transaction. These technologies let you navigate the ever-changing digital marketplace with confidence, knowing your sensitive information is wrapped in layers of protection. Whether you're buying a cup of coffee or a new laptop, understanding how your data is kept safe enhances your experience, allowing you to enjoy the conveniences of modern life without fear. Your financial security is too valuable to leave to chance, so arm yourself with the knowledge needed to confidently navigate the cashless world.

Your Role in Security: Tips on Protecting Yourself During Transactions

In our current world of online shopping, we enjoy incredible convenience at our fingertips. With just a few clicks or taps on our smartphones, we can order just about anything, from groceries to the latest gadgets. While this ease of shopping is fantastic, it also brings along new challenges and risks. As users of digital payment methods, we must recognize our responsibility in keeping our transactions safe. Given how common cybercrime has become, it's vital to take steps to protect our financial well-being.

Imagine walking through a lively market filled with colorful stalls and cheerful vendors trying to sell their wares. You spot a gorgeous handcrafted item that catches your eye, but as you pull out your wallet, you notice a few suspicious-looking characters hanging around. This situation mirrors the risks you face in online shopping. Just like you'd stay alert in a crowded market, it's just as important to be cautious when you're shopping online.

One of the first things you can do to improve your security is to create strong passwords. Think of your password as the lock on your front door. A weak lock can be easily broken, but a strong one can keep even the most determined intruder out. Strong passwords should be a mix of letters, numbers, and special characters, avoiding easy-to-guess options like "123456" or "password." Instead, try using a phrase or a string of random words that only you would understand—like "BlueElephantDances@Midnight."

Also, steer clear of using the same password for multiple accounts. If a hacker gets into one of your accounts, they could easily use that same password to break into others. This is where password managers can be really helpful. They securely store your various passwords and can even create strong ones for you. Think of it as having a super-secure vault for your valuable keys, so you don't have to memorize each one.

Next up is two-factor authentication (2FA). You can think of this extra layer of security as having a bouncer at your digital door. Even if a hacker gets hold of your password, they still need a second piece of information to get in. This might be a code sent to your phone or an app that gives you temporary access codes. By turning on 2FA for your accounts, you set up an important barrier against unauthorized access, making it much harder for intruders to get through.

While you navigate the online world, it's crucial to stay alert about the sites you visit. A common trap is falling for phishing scams where criminals pretend to be trustworthy businesses to trick you into giving away personal information. Picture receiving an email from a well-known vendor saying there's a "problem" with your account, urging you to click a link that leads to a fake site designed to steal your details. Always check the sender's email address and the link before you click. If anything seems off, go directly to the official website or reach out to customer support for verification.

It's also smart to make sure you're shopping on secure websites. Look for "HTTPS" in the URL; the "S" means "secure," indicating that the site is using encryption to protect your data. Plus, if you see a padlock icon in the address bar, that's a good sign that the site is taking steps to keep your information safe. If you encounter a site that only has "HTTP," think carefully before entering any personal or financial data.

When you shop online, using reputable payment gateways can provide extra security. Services like PayPal or Stripe act as a buffer, making sure your sensitive information is shielded from the seller. Using these platforms means you don't have to give your credit card details to every vendor you buy from. Instead, the payment service handles the transaction securely, much like using a trusted courier to carry a valuable package for you instead of handing it to a stranger.

Another good tip is to consider using virtual credit cards for your online shopping. Many banks offer this feature, which creates a temporary card number linked to your actual account. This way, you limit the risk of exposing your real card details if there's a data breach. It's like wearing a disguise while shopping in a busy market; you can enjoy the experience without revealing your true identity to potential threats.

Don't forget to keep your devices and software updated. Regular updates help protect you from the latest online threats and vulnerabilities. Software developers work hard to fix security issues, and not updating can leave you open to attacks, just like neglecting to repair a broken lock on your door.

Using reliable security software is another way to keep yourself safe. Antivirus programs scan for harmful software, while firewalls create a barrier between your computer and possible threats from outside. Choosing a trustworthy security solution that fits your needs can give you an edge in fighting off attacks, much like having a guard watching over your home.

As you make online purchases, remember to check your financial accounts regularly. Keeping an eye on your bank and credit card statements helps you catch any unauthorized charges quickly. If you see something suspicious, report it to your bank immediately. Just like you would take action if you spotted a thief in that busy market, being proactive about any shady activity can help you minimize potential losses.

Education is a key aspect of keeping secure. As a smart shopper, it's important to stay updated about new threats and common scams. Consider subscribing to newsletters or following trustworthy sources that can keep you informed. Knowing about the latest tricks used by fraudsters helps you spot and steer clear of potential dangers.

Also, be cautious when using public Wi-Fi networks. While it can be tempting to connect while relaxing at your favorite café, these networks might be unsafe and attract hackers. Think about using a virtual private network (VPN) to encrypt your internet connection when accessing sensitive sites on public networks. A VPN provides a secure tunnel, safeguarding your data from prying eyes.

Finally, listen to your intuition. If something feels wrong, it probably is. If a deal appears too good to be true, trust your instincts and walk away. Scammers often take advantage of people's excitement and urge to act quickly, so taking a moment to reassess can save you from making poor choices.

As we navigate the digital landscape, it's crucial to take ownership of our safety during transactions. By creating strong passwords, enabling two-factor authentication, using secure websites, and staying alert to scams, we play an active role in protecting ourselves financially.

Understanding the technology that helps secure our transactions, like encryption and tokenization, allows us to appreciate the complexities behind cashless payments and empowers us to take control of our safety.

Ultimately, while online shopping brings unparalleled convenience, it's up to us to ensure our transactions stay secure. By following these best practices and keeping ourselves informed, we can confidently explore the vast world of digital shopping, enjoying all its perks without fear. So, the next time you make a purchase, remember that your security is not just about technology; it's also about your actions and habits. Step into the role of protector of your financial information, and enjoy the digital marketplace knowing you're safe and secure.

Chapter 8: Regulations and Standards—The Rules of the Game

Governing Bodies: The Guardians of Payment Systems

Imagine walking into a lively sports arena, where the atmosphere is electric and fans are cheering for their favorite teams. In the midst of all this excitement, the referees stand out, keeping a close watch on the game to ensure fair play and adherence to the rules. In the realm of financial transactions, governing bodies play a similar role; they act like the referees for the payment systems that support our cashless society. Though often overlooked, these organizations are vital for maintaining the integrity and security of financial exchanges, providing guidance and oversight to everyone involved.

At the forefront of these guardians is the Payment Card Industry Security Standards Council (PCI SSC). Founded in 2006, this council consists of major credit card companies, including Visa, MasterCard, American Express, Discover, and JCB. The PCI SSC was created in response to the rising number of data breaches and the urgent need for a unified set of security standards to protect sensitive payment card information. They introduced the Payment Card Industry Data

Security Standard (PCI DSS), a thorough framework aimed at bolstering card transaction security.

The PCI DSS acts as a crucial guide for merchants, service providers, and financial institutions to follow. It includes twelve requirements that cover a wide range of security measures, from maintaining a secure network to applying strong access controls. For example, one requirement insists on encrypting cardholder data during transmission, ensuring that sensitive information doesn't fall into the wrong hands. Following these standards isn't just about ticking a box; it's a promise to protect consumers and build trust in payment systems. Ignoring these rules can lead to serious consequences, including hefty fines and losing the ability to process card payments.

Now, picture a merchant whose point-of-sale system gets hacked, putting thousands of customers' credit card details at risk. The fallout would be immediate and devastating, resulting in not just financial loss but also lasting damage to the merchant's reputation. By following the PCI DSS, merchants can take proactive steps to protect themselves from such disasters and become active participants in creating a secure transaction environment. This commitment to security helps build consumer trust, encouraging more people to engage in cashless transactions.

While the PCI SSC mainly focuses on the payment card industry, the world of financial regulations is much broader, with various governing bodies overseeing different aspects of the financial system. One key player in the United States is the Federal Financial Institutions Examination Council (FFIEC). Established in 1979, this interagency body includes several federal regulatory agencies, such as the Office of the Comptroller of the Currency, the Federal Reserve, and the Federal Deposit Insurance Corporation. The main mission of the FFIEC is to set standards for examining financial institutions, ensuring that banks and credit unions operate safely and soundly.

The FFIEC provides guidelines for risk management and fraud protection, creating a framework that financial institutions must follow. For instance, they stress the necessity of regular risk assessments to identify any potential weaknesses. They also recommend implementing robust anti-fraud measures, like multi-factor authentication and transaction monitoring. By laying down these standards, the FFIEC not only strengthens the resilience of financial institutions but also helps protect consumers from the risks associated with online banking and digital transactions.

Think of the FFIEC as a sports referee who constantly reviews the game, ensuring everyone plays by the rules and stepping in when necessary. Just as a referee might issue a warning to a player for unsportsmanlike conduct, the FFIEC holds banks accountable for their actions, fostering an environment of compliance and integrity. When consumers transact with a bank that follows FFIEC guidelines, they can feel more secure knowing their money is protected by strict standards and oversight.

Looking beyond the U.S., we find the Financial Action Task Force (FATF), an intergovernmental organization founded in 1989 to tackle money laundering and terrorism financing. The FATF creates recommendations and guidelines that help countries develop strong frameworks to safeguard their financial systems from illegal activities. Through mutual evaluations, the FATF checks how well member countries comply with its standards, encouraging nations to adopt best practices to fight financial crime.

The FATF's impact is significant, with its guidelines being embraced by various jurisdictions worldwide. This has led to a patchwork of compliance measures aimed at addressing financial crime. For example, they highlight the importance of customer due diligence, requiring financial institutions to verify the identity of their clients and keep an eye on their transactions for any suspicious activity. By putting these measures in place, the FATF aims to create a united front against the threats posed by money laundering and terrorist financing.

In many ways, the FATF acts like a global referee, ensuring that countries follow the same rules in the battle against financial crime. By promoting international cooperation and standardization, the FATF builds trust among nations, making it much harder for criminals to take advantage of loopholes. When consumers are aware that financial institutions are monitored by an international governing body, they're more likely to engage in cross-border transactions, feeling reassured by the security measures in place.

The comparison to referees goes beyond simple oversight; it also underscores the intricate relationship between governing bodies and the stakeholders they oversee. Merchants and financial institutions must navigate a complex web of regulations, balancing compliance with their business goals. The challenge is realizing that these regulations aren't just obstacles; they are essential parts that contribute to the overall health and integrity of the payment ecosystem.

Think back to the sports world, where players might occasionally complain about the strictness of the rules. However, it's the presence of these rules that ensures fair play and protects the integrity of the game. In the financial sector, regulations set by governing bodies like the PCI SSC, FFIEC, and FATF are crafted to create a level playing field where trust and security can thrive. By following these standards, merchants not only protect their businesses but also foster a culture of security that benefits everyone in the transaction process.

As we navigate the complex landscape of payment systems, it becomes clear that the role of governing bodies is vital. They act as guardians of the payment ecosystem, ensuring that transactions happen securely and fairly. By setting and enforcing standards, these regulatory bodies help to build confidence among consumers, merchants, and financial institutions alike. In a world that increasingly relies on digital payments, the significance of these guardians is more important than ever.

Ultimately, the relationship between consumers and the payment systems they use is built on trust, and this trust is nurtured by the hard work of regulatory bodies. Just as fans cheer for their teams, they also want to feel secure in their choices, knowing that the game is being played fairly. The PCI SSC, FFIEC, and FATF are the unsung heroes of the financial world, tirelessly working to create an environment where safe and efficient transactions can flourish. This dedication to oversight, compliance, and security is what keeps the rules of the game intact.

Compliance Matters: The Importance of Adhering to Guidelines

In the intricate world of financial transactions, compliance is more than just a necessity; it's a lifeline. Picture a ship sailing through rocky waters: without a dependable compass and a clear map, the captain risks disaster. Likewise, merchants and banks that ignore established guidelines are putting themselves in jeopardy. The realm of financial compliance is filled with cautionary tales of data breaches, hefty fines, and damage to reputations—all resulting from not playing by the rules.

Take, for example, the notorious Target data breach of 2013. Hackers accessed the credit and debit card information of more than 40 million customers, along with the personal details of an additional 70 million. This incident, which resulted from poor security measures, cost Target an estimated $162 million in losses and seriously damaged customer trust. Suddenly, shoppers were hesitant to swipe their cards at checkout, fearing their information could end up in the hands of criminals. This situation serves as a powerful reminder that not following security standards can lead to devastating consequences—affecting not just profits but the very relationships businesses have with their customers.

The fallout from non-compliance goes well beyond financial losses. Once a company experiences a major data breach, it often spirals into a cycle of panic, blame, and damage control. The public's reaction usually triggers a storm of negative headlines; stakeholders grow nervous, and customers may leave in droves. In a world where trust is everything, the long-term fallout from such incidents can severely harm a company's reputation. The takeaway is simple: compliance isn't just another task on a to-do list; it's a critical piece of keeping a healthy business running.

Regulatory frameworks are the backbone of compliance, outlining the rules that merchants and financial institutions must follow. One of the most important regulations shaping data protection today is the General Data Protection Regulation, or GDPR. Introduced in 2018, this European Union law stands as a strong advocate for data privacy, setting strict standards for protecting personal information. For businesses that operate within or deal with clients in the EU, compliance isn't optional; it's the law. Under GDPR, organizations must take various steps, like getting clear consent from consumers before handling their data and ensuring that information is stored securely. Ignoring these regulations can lead to fines reaching up to 4% of annual global turnover or €20 million—whichever amount is higher.

The effects of GDPR aren't limited to Europe. Companies around the globe need to adjust their practices to meet its tough requirements, no matter where they're located.

For instance, American companies that deal with EU citizens' data have to navigate the complexities of GDPR compliance. This has pushed many businesses to pour significant resources into revamping their data management systems, creating privacy policies, and training staff on new protocols. Not recognizing the importance of these regulations is like sailing into a storm without a life jacket; the risks are simply too significant to overlook.

Another vital regulation in the compliance puzzle is the Sarbanes-Oxley Act (SOX), which was enacted in the U.S. following the corporate scandals of the early 2000s, like Enron and WorldCom. SOX is designed to protect investors by enhancing the accuracy and reliability of corporate disclosures. A key principle of this law is financial transparency, which requires publicly traded companies to stick to strict reporting standards. The act compels organizations to set up internal controls and procedures for financial reporting, promoting accountability.

The influence of SOX goes beyond just accounting; it acts as a deterrent against corporate fraud and mismanagement. By holding executives responsible for the accuracy of financial statements, SOX helps build trust among investors. Failure to follow SOX guidelines can bring severe penalties, including substantial fines, criminal charges, and even jail time for corporate leaders. This law emphasizes that compliance isn't just a bureaucratic hurdle; it's a crucial part of maintaining trust and integrity in financial markets.

As businesses navigate the complexities of compliance, they need to take proactive measures to ensure they're following regulations. Regular audits are essential for checking compliance levels and spotting areas that need improvement. Think of audits like routine health check-ups for your business; just as a doctor examines a patient's health to catch potential problems early, audits help organizations assess their compliance status and fix issues before they turn into crises.

Training employees is also a key aspect of compliance efforts. Too often, breaches happen not because someone wanted to cause harm but due to a lack of understanding of the rules. By teaching employees about regulatory requirements and best practices, businesses can create a culture of compliance that spreads throughout the organization. Training should be an ongoing effort, continuously adapting to changes in regulations. Think of it like a sports team sharpening its skills; regular practice and reinforcement of strategies are vital for victory.

In addition to training and audits, businesses must stay alert by updating their security protocols. The digital world is always changing, as are the tactics used by cybercriminals. Consistently updating security measures, like applying software patches and enhancing data encryption, is crucial for protecting sensitive information. Falling behind in technological advancements leaves organizations vulnerable to threats. In this sense, compliance isn't a final destination but a continuous journey—one that requires watchfulness, flexibility, and a commitment to ongoing improvement.

Often, compliance is seen as a burden, a series of obstacles that businesses must overcome to operate legally. However, it's important to highlight the benefits of following guidelines. By viewing compliance as a fundamental part of their operations, organizations can not only reduce risks but also boost their reputation. Consumers are increasingly drawn to businesses that prioritize data privacy and security. By showing a commitment to compliance, organizations can build trust, foster customer loyalty, and stand out in a competitive marketplace.

Regulations like GDPR and SOX serve a twofold purpose: protecting consumers and creating a fair playing field for businesses. When organizations adhere to these rules, they help cultivate a fair and competitive marketplace where companies can succeed without resorting to unethical practices. Therefore, compliance isn't just about dodging penalties; it's an investment in the long-term health of the business.

As we see a growing reliance on digital transactions, the stakes have never been higher. The world of compliance is constantly changing, and businesses must stay nimble to keep up with new regulations and emerging threats. The dedication to compliance will mold the future of financial transactions, ensuring that trust and security remain central to consumer experiences.

In this light, merchants and financial institutions are not merely players in the game; they are caretakers of the system. By following established guidelines, they help uphold the integrity of the payment ecosystem, ultimately benefiting both consumers and the wider economy. The significance of compliance cannot be emphasized enough; it is the foundation upon which trust is built, a necessary condition for the growth of cashless transactions in our digital age.

Impact on Consumers: Shielding Users and Shaping Experiences

In today's world, where tapping a smartphone or swiping a card can send money anywhere in an instant, keeping these transactions safe is more important than ever. The digital payment landscape is always changing, offering both convenience and risks. Regulations in this space act like guardrails, not just to keep things orderly, but also to enrich the overall experience for consumers navigating this cashless environment.

Think about what it's like to shop online. You're on your favorite store's website, and you spot those perfect shoes. With just a click, you add them to your cart and move to checkout. As you enter your payment info, there's a little flutter of anxiety—are your details safe? If the retailer follows strong regulations and uses tight data protection measures, you can breathe easier. These regulations help shield your personal information with advanced data encryption, creating a protective barrier around your sensitive data that keeps cybercriminals at bay.

Data encryption is a powerful tool that changes your readable info into a code that's nearly impossible for anyone without the right key to understand. Imagine your payment details as a secret message; only a select few can decode it. While "encryption" might sound daunting, it simply means that if someone were to intercept your payment info, they'd just see a jumble of nonsense. This security measure builds trust between consumers and businesses, letting shoppers participate in cashless transactions without fear.

But data encryption is just one piece of the puzzle when it comes to protecting consumers during their shopping experiences. Fraud detection systems, equipped with smart algorithms, act like vigilant guardians, constantly monitoring every transaction for signs of trouble. These systems look for unusual patterns and behaviors, using machine learning and artificial intelligence to highlight anything that seems off. Imagine having a personal protector who knows your usual buying habits. If they spot something strange—like a big purchase in a country you've never visited—they raise a red flag.

This means that if you accidentally leave your card unattended, these systems will likely catch any unauthorized charges before they escalate. This proactive approach not only helps prevent financial losses for consumers but also eases the worries that often come with cashless payments. Knowing there are protective measures in place allows people to enjoy the convenience of digital payments while feeling secure about their financial information.

However, even with strong data encryption and fraud detection systems, misunderstandings can still happen. Regulations step in here, providing consumers with safety nets like chargebacks, which allow people to dispute unauthorized transactions. Picture this: you ordered those shoes, but instead, a pair of socks arrives—or nothing at all. With the chargeback process, you can recover your money by contesting the charge with your bank. This feature empowers buyers, ensuring they have options if something goes wrong.

Chargebacks aren't just about fixing problems; they also help deter fraud and keep everyone accountable in the financial system.

Retailers know they need to be extra careful with transactions since consumers can challenge any mistakes. This creates a healthier marketplace where both buyers and sellers work together with honesty.

So, regulations serve as a stabilizing force that helps build trust in the financial system. As consumers navigate the world of cashless payments, these regulations reassure them that their needs are a priority. They don't view regulations as mere red tape; they see them as vital protections that enhance their shopping experiences and give them peace of mind.

Plus, the positive effects of regulations reach far beyond individual transactions. As people gain more trust in the payment system, they're more likely to use digital payments, which helps boost economic growth. When folks feel secure using cashless methods, they tend to spend more, investing in goods and services that fuel the economy. This interconnected web of trust, security, and economic activity showcases the crucial role that regulations play in cultivating a successful financial landscape.

Let's take a moment to think about a small business owner who has recently started using digital payment solutions. At first, they were nervous about accepting credit cards or mobile payments because of their fears about fraud or chargebacks. But once they understood the regulatory protections available, they began to embrace cashless payment options. Over time, they noticed a change—customers were more willing to make purchases, and sales began to rise.

This small business owner found themselves in a win-win situation. Not only did they appreciate the ease of cashless transactions, but they also saw an increase in revenue. Consumers enjoyed a smooth shopping experience, reassured by regulations designed to protect them. This example highlights how regulations can create a ripple effect, promoting security and confidence across the financial system.

As we continue to explore how consumer protection unfolds in the cashless world, it's worth remembering that regulations are not set in stone. They evolve alongside technology and the shifting needs of consumers. Regulatory bodies must stay alert and flexible, frequently evaluating new threats and ensuring that rules keep up with changes in payment systems. This ongoing connection between regulations and technology is vital for creating a secure space for both consumers and businesses.

Throughout this changing landscape, educating consumers remains a top priority. As regulations shift and new technologies emerge, people must stay informed about their rights and the protections available to them. Financial education can help individuals grasp how cashless transactions work, the significance of data security, and how to protect themselves. When consumers are informed, they become empowered participants in the financial system, ready to make smart choices.

In a world where digital transactions are the norm, the importance of regulations is clear. They aren't just a bunch of rules and guidelines; they are the building blocks that protect consumers and shape their experiences. By fostering trust and encouraging the responsible use of cashless systems, regulations help create a thriving financial landscape for everyone.

Looking ahead, it's evident that the relationship between consumers, businesses, and regulatory bodies will keep changing. As we rely more on digital transactions, the commitment to protecting consumers will continue to be a top priority. Through these efforts, we can uphold the integrity of the financial system, nurturing a safe space where individuals can confidently engage in cashless transactions without fear. The ultimate goal is to establish a system where consumers can take advantage of modern payment solutions, knowing their interests are safeguarded by strong regulations designed to enhance their experiences in the digital marketplace.

Walter Bancroft

Chapter 9: Global Payments—Transactions Without Borders

Currency Conversion

Let's picture this: you're getting ready for a fantastic trip across Europe. After months of saving up, you have a nice stack of cash in your home currency, thinking about the delicious croissants in Paris, the creamy gelato in Rome, and maybe a pint in London. But as you stroll through the lively streets of France, it hits you—your dollars won't help you much until you turn them into euros. Although it seems like a simple task, converting your money isn't as easy as it sounds. Think of it like trading one kind of ticket for another at an amusement park; the value of your ticket can change based on the park's popularity, or in this case, the economic factors affecting the currency.

When you approach the currency exchange booth, the bright lights and vibrant signs that shout "Lowest Rates!" grab your attention. But wait a minute! Before you hand over your hard-earned money, let's break down what currency conversion really means and how it affects your spending while you travel.

At its heart, currency conversion is simply swapping one kind of money for another based on the current exchange rate. This rate is never fixed; it goes up and down, influenced by many factors like economic conditions, political stability, and even market guesses. So, when you find yourself at that kiosk with your dollars ready to trade, keep in mind that the rate you see might not be the same when your transaction goes through. The thrill of picking out the perfect souvenir or enjoying a scrumptious meal can quickly fade if you're taken by surprise by unexpected costs.

To navigate this process, it's key to understand how exchange rates work. They're set by a complex mix of different factors. For example, take interest rates. When a country raises its interest rates, it often draws in foreign money looking for better returns, which increases demand for that country's currency and can make it more valuable compared to others. On the flip side, if a country experiences high inflation, its currency may lose value, making it less attractive to foreign investors.

Central banks are crucial players in this intricate game. They keep an eye on their country's economy and may step in to stabilize their currency in the foreign exchange market. They do this by buying or selling currency reserves or changing interest rates. Most of the trading happens in the interbank market, where banks buy and sell currencies among themselves. These transactions can influence the rates you see at local exchange offices or online currency services.

During your travels, you might notice the exchange rate shifting from one minute to the next. For instance, you could see that 1 dollar equals 0.85 euros at one moment, and just a few hours later, it drops to 0.83 euros. These changes can directly affect how much you can spend. If you're looking at a $100 meal in France, the price in euros can swing quite a bit depending on when you convert your money. If the rate is 0.85, your meal would cost around 85 euros. But if it falls to 0.83, you'll be paying 100 euros instead— a difference of 15 euros, which could easily buy you a nice bottle of wine to enjoy with your meal.

Now that we have a better understanding of how exchange rates work, let's shift gears to the practical side of converting currency. Once you land in a foreign country, you have a few different options for converting your money, each with its own pros and cons. You can use banks, currency exchange offices, or credit cards, and it's smart to think through each choice.

Banks are usually a safe bet, especially for larger amounts of cash. They generally offer competitive rates, and their fees can be lower compared to exchange kiosks. However, if you're short on time or only need to exchange a little bit, waiting in line at a bank might not be the best option.

Currency exchange offices, typically found at airports, tourist spots, and downtown areas, give you quick access to cash. However, they often come with higher fees and not-so-great rates compared to banks. It's wise to look past the flashy signs claiming "best rates" and check the fine print. These offices often make their money through hidden fees, which can seriously cut into the amount of foreign currency you end up with.

Using a credit card can also be a convenient way to handle currency conversion. Many credit card companies provide competitive exchange rates, and transactions are usually processed using real-time rates, which is beneficial. Still, be cautious about possible foreign transaction fees, which can range from 1% to 3% of the total cost. Some credit cards, especially travel rewards cards, waive these fees, making them a solid choice for frequent travelers. Before you head out, it's a good idea to check with your bank or credit card provider to know the specific terms for using your card abroad.

As you think through your options for converting currency, don't forget to check the current exchange rates before you make any trades. There are plenty of online tools and mobile apps that can give you up-to-date information. By equipping yourself with this knowledge, you can make smarter choices and possibly save a good amount of money during your trip.

Let's say you're planning to spend a weekend in Paris and expect to use about $500. Before you set off, take a peek at the current exchange rate. If it's looking good, you might decide to exchange a larger sum upfront. On the other hand, if the rate isn't favorable, you could opt to change just enough to cover your first few days and keep an eye out for better rates as your trip goes on.

So, currency conversion isn't just a necessary chore; it's a key part of your travel experience. The more you learn about how it works, the more confident you'll feel navigating different countries, currencies, and cultures. It's all about making the most of your money while enjoying the amazing experiences that travel brings. After all, those unforgettable meals, stunning sights, and cherished memories are worth every penny—if you approach currency conversion smartly.

Cross-Border Fees and Considerations: Navigating the Costs of Global Transactions

Imagine yourself at a charming restaurant, ready to dive into a delicious meal. You've perused the menu, chosen that mouthwatering dish you've been dreaming about, and called over the waiter to place your order. But as you take your first bite, confusion creeps in when the bill arrives. The price you saw on the menu doesn't match what you're seeing now. There's an extra charge for tax, another for tip, and suddenly, the meal that felt like a steal turns into a financial sting. This scenario—those unexpected extra charges that catch diners off guard—reflects what happens in cross-border transactions. Just like you need to keep an eye out for the real cost of dining out, the same goes for international purchases, where hidden fees can lead to unwelcome surprises.

When you engage in cross-border transactions, whether it's buying a beautiful silk scarf in Venice or reserving a hotel room in Bangkok, you might face a range of fees that can eat into your budget and turn your spending plan into mere wishful thinking. Grasping these hidden costs is the first step toward making sense of the complicated world of global transactions. At the top of this list are foreign transaction fees, often popping up when you use a credit card outside your home country. These fees can range anywhere from a small 1% to a hefty 3% of each transaction, sneaking into your total like uninvited guests at a party.

Alongside foreign transaction fees, many travelers also run into dynamic currency conversion (DCC). Picture this: you're in a foreign land, making a purchase, and the seller offers to charge you in your home currency instead of the local one. It sounds like a great deal—who wouldn't want to see exactly how much they're spending in dollars without tackling euro conversions on the fly? But beware, this convenience often comes with a much higher price tag than you expect. DCC can inflate your costs due to less favorable exchange rates set by the merchant, turning what seems like a simple transaction into something far pricier. Understanding DCC is key, as it could save you from stepping into this costly pitfall.

So, you might be asking: how do you dodge these hidden fees and keep more of your hard-earned money where it belongs? The answer lies in smart planning and picking the right financial tools. Opting for credit cards that don't charge foreign transaction fees is a wise choice for international travelers. Many credit card companies understand the needs of those who travel frequently and offer cards with features that can save you significant money over time. Moreover, withdrawing cash in the local currency usually gives you a better exchange rate than what you'll get at a currency exchange booth or through DCC.

But understanding cross-border fees isn't just about credit card companies. The payment method you choose can greatly affect the total cost you face. For instance, if you're thinking about using a debit card for your international purchases, double-check to see if your bank assesses foreign transaction fees.

Some banks tack on their own fees in addition to what the merchant might charge, which can double the hit to your wallet.

Additionally, whether you opt for cash or credit can also affect how much you spend overseas. While cash can help you steer clear of certain fees entirely, it comes with its own challenges. Carrying a lot of cash can feel risky, and it may not be accepted for bigger purchases. Planning ahead to identify which payment method works best for your travel needs is crucial—after all, the goal is to enjoy your journey without being weighed down by unnecessary costs.

In today's digital age, online wallets have become a popular choice for making payments abroad. Services like PayPal, Venmo, and Apple Pay offer convenience, but they come with their own sets of fees worth examining. Currency conversion fees and transaction costs linked with these platforms can pile up quickly, especially if you use them frequently. Just because you're using technology doesn't guarantee you're getting the best deal. Doing your homework on the fee structures of these digital services can help you avoid unpleasant surprises.

As we navigate through the world of global transactions, it's a good idea to think beyond just the individual fees and consider how your financial choices impact your overall budget. Every transaction you make while traveling can affect your total expenses. For example, if you're journeying through several countries on a tight budget, every little fee adds up, and could force you to cut back on experiences you were looking forward to—like enjoying a meal at that delightful café or buying a unique piece of art.

Another factor to keep in mind is how fluctuating exchange rates can affect the fees you incur. If you've ever tried to convert currency, you know that exchange rates can shift dramatically from day to day, or even hour to hour. This fluctuation can change the prices of goods and the fees tied to them. Timing your purchases, when you can, can make a big difference. While you might not have the luxury of waiting for the perfect moment to snag that leather jacket in Florence, being aware of the rates and fees related to your transactions can empower you to make smarter choices.

As you navigate this complex world of cross-border fees and considerations, remember that being informed is your strongest tool. Just like a savvy diner checks for hidden charges on the menu, you can equip yourself with knowledge that helps you steer clear of unexpected costs during your international travels. By being proactive about understanding fees, choosing the best payment methods, and keeping an eye on exchange rates, you can transform your trip from one that feels financially burdensome into one that's enjoyable and memorable.

To illustrate these points, let's consider a scenario. Picture yourself getting ready for a two-week adventure across Europe with a budget of $5,000. As you plan your itinerary, you focus on the experiences that matter most to you, whether that's exploring the vibrant streets of Barcelona or having a romantic getaway in Paris. However, while you're arranging everything, you forget to factor in the various fees and costs tied to your transactions. If you were to incur just a 2% foreign transaction fee on your credit card purchases, that could potentially whittle away $100 of your budget—money that could have gone toward creating an unforgettable memory.

Ultimately, navigating the costs of global transactions isn't just about convenience; it requires careful attention, smart planning, and a bit of savvy decision-making. By grasping the types of fees that might be lurking in your financial interactions, you'll be better prepared to manage your spending and truly enjoy your international adventures. So, whether you're indulging in a culinary delight abroad or exploring a lively market, stay aware and informed—because every dollar counts when it comes to enriching your travel experiences.

The Future of International Payments

Thinking about the future of international payments creates a sense of excitement, similar to the thrill of visiting a new country and immersing yourself in its lively culture. As technology moves forward at lightning speed, the way we handle money across borders is changing in ways that once seemed like something out of a sci-fi story. The rise of digital nomads—those adventurous people who work remotely while traveling the world—illustrates this exciting shift. They effortlessly navigate global commerce thanks to innovations that are changing how money flows around the globe.

Picture a digital nomad named Alex, relaxing in a sun-drenched café in Bali with a laptop open and a coconut in hand, managing clients from every corner of the world. With just a few clicks, Alex can send money to a web developer in India, receive payment from a client in Canada, and pay for a local tour guide—all without breaking a sweat. No longer bound by traditional banking hours or physical locations, this modern worker represents a shift toward a more flexible and accessible financial world. This world, powered by technology, is designed to make international payments as easy as ordering your favorite coffee.

As we think about what's ahead, it's clear that several exciting changes are driving this new age of global transactions. The digital revolution has given life to a wide range of tools and platforms that make international payments faster, safer, and simpler. From cryptocurrencies to blockchain technology, these innovations hold the promise of connecting distant economies and empowering both individuals and businesses to take control of their financial activities.

Cryptocurrencies have emerged as a game-changer in this field. Once dismissed as a fleeting trend, they are now being taken seriously by investors, businesses, and even governments. These digital currencies, built on blockchain technology, offer major benefits compared to traditional banking. One of the most attractive features is their potential to significantly lower transaction costs. In a world where sending money internationally can feel like navigating a confusing maze filled with fees and exchange rates, cryptocurrencies serve as a refreshing option.

Take remittances, for example—a crucial support system for millions of families worldwide. Traditionally, sending money home can come with high fees and long processing times, which can take a big chunk out of the sender's hard-earned money. However, as cryptocurrencies like Bitcoin gain popularity, this situation is starting to change. Think about Maria, who sends money to her family in Guatemala. By using a cryptocurrency platform, she can quickly transfer funds without the steep fees tied to traditional banks, ensuring that her family receives the full amount she intended without any delays.

Blockchain technology, which is the backbone of cryptocurrencies, acts as a secure record that keeps track of all transactions with remarkable transparency. This feature not only strengthens security but also helps to cut down on fraud—an ever-present worry in the financial world. In addition to remittances, businesses are beginning to look at cryptocurrencies for cross-border payments, speeding up processes that previously took days.

Real-life examples are everywhere. Companies like Overstock and Newegg have embraced cryptocurrencies, allowing customers to shop using Bitcoin. The ease of these transactions, along with the possibility of lower fees, makes this an appealing choice for both buyers and sellers. Being able to bypass traditional banks and their associated costs can be a huge advantage for small businesses hoping to grow internationally.

That said, the path to wide-scale cryptocurrency acceptance isn't without its challenges. Regulatory uncertainties and fluctuating prices create hurdles that need careful navigation. Plus, many consumers are still cautious, unsure about how to engage with this new financial landscape. Education and understanding will be key to helping people accept these innovations, bridging the gap between doubt and trust.

As we explore what's to come in international payments, we can't overlook the role of digital wallets and fintech solutions that are making global commerce more accessible than ever. Gone are the days of needing to go to the bank or deal with complicated wire transfers to send money across borders. Digital wallets—like PayPal, Venmo, and a host of new platforms—are changing the game by providing fast and user-friendly options.

Think about the convenience of a digital wallet. With just a smartphone and an internet connection, you can send or receive money at the touch of a button. For example, imagine you're at a lively market in Mexico and want to buy a beautifully crafted item. Instead of searching for cash or grappling with a confusing exchange rate, you can simply pay using your digital wallet. The transaction is instant, and you can relax knowing your payment is safe.

The rise of fintech has also sparked innovations tailored to the needs of international consumers. Services like TransferWise (now known as Wise) have emerged as alternatives to traditional banks, offering real-time exchange rates and straightforward, low fees. Whether you're an expatriate sending money home or a traveler needing to exchange currency, these platforms provide unmatched convenience and value.

However, while digital wallets and fintech solutions make global transactions easier, they also have their own concerns. Security remains a top priority. As cyber threats evolve, the need for strong protections against fraud and hacking is more crucial than ever. Users need to stay alert, using strong passwords, enabling two-factor authentication, and keeping up-to-date on potential risks.

Another important factor to consider is how different platforms compare to traditional banking methods. While digital wallets typically offer lower fees and quicker processing times, some people argue that the personal touch and security provided by physical banks shouldn't be ignored. Finding the right balance between the convenience of fintech and the dependability of traditional banking is a personal choice that will vary from person to person.

With all these changes happening, it's natural to wonder how they will affect individual spending habits and international transactions. For many, the idea of handling finances in real-time without geographical limits is liberating. Imagine being able to buy that stunning piece of jewelry from a small artisan in Thailand, knowing that your payment will go through instantly and without hassle. The world starts to feel a little smaller as purchasing power crosses borders.

Yet, to fully embrace these changes, one must take a proactive stance. The financial landscape is shifting, and those who stay informed will be better equipped to navigate this exciting new world. Keeping up with the latest advancements, understanding how new payment methods can benefit you, and being mindful of potential risks are all crucial steps in this journey.

As you witness the rapid progress in international payments, it's clear that the future is brimming with possibilities. The blend of technology, consumer needs, and financial creativity is opening doors to a new era where cross-border transactions are not just feasible but also more efficient and user-friendly than ever before. The ability to send and receive money globally with ease empowers both individuals and businesses.

In short, the world of international payments is on the brink of a major transformation. As digital nomads flourish and new technologies emerge, the way we interact with money will keep evolving. Embracing these changes means being open to the financial tools available and recognizing their potential to enrich your global experiences. Whether you're a traveler, a business owner, or simply curious about the financial world, staying educated and adaptable will serve you well in this fast-changing environment.

The future is filled with both opportunities and challenges, and it's up to us to make the most of it. By keeping an eye on innovations in international payments, we can empower ourselves and others to navigate this exciting landscape, ensuring that our connections with the global economy are as rewarding as our journeys around the world. Each transaction becomes a part of the ever-expanding network of global commerce, where the possibilities are as vast as our imaginations.

Walter Bancroft

Chapter 10: The Road Ahead—Innovations Shaping Payments

AI and Machine Learning: Enhancing Fraud Detection and Customer Experience

Imagine strolling through a lively marketplace, where vendors are enthusiastically promoting their daily specials and customers are bartering for the best prices. The atmosphere buzzes with laughter, the air is filled with the aroma of fresh produce, and you can hear the cheerful sound of coins clinking as they change hands. Now, picture that vibrant scene in the digital world, where transactions happen at lightning speed and the stakes are higher than ever. In this new landscape, where cash has largely given way to credit cards, mobile wallets, and other electronic payments, security and customer satisfaction are more crucial than ever. Enter artificial intelligence and machine learning—like superheroes in the world of financial technology—ready to tackle fraud and improve the customer experience.

AI and machine learning aren't just trendy terms thrown around in tech conversations; they are the forces transforming the future of payment systems. With cybercrime becoming more clever and advanced, it's vital for businesses to keep up and protect themselves and their customers. Today's fraudsters use intricate schemes that can easily bypass old-fashioned security measures, making it essential for payment platforms to change and adapt quickly. By tapping into the power of AI and machine learning, companies are not just strengthening their defenses; they are also rethinking how customers connect with their services.

At its heart, AI is all about mimicking human intelligence. Machine learning, a part of AI, enables systems to learn from data patterns and improve their abilities over time without needing specific instructions for every situation. This learning and adapting capability is what makes these technologies so good at spotting fraud. Traditional fraud detection systems often rely on fixed rules and thresholds, which can be too rigid and ineffective against the constantly changing tactics used by fraudsters. In contrast, machine learning algorithms can sift through vast amounts of transaction data in real time, spotting unusual patterns and highlighting suspicious activity with impressive accuracy.

For example, think about a payment processing company using machine learning algorithms to keep an eye on transactions. Instead of just depending on past data and a "one size fits all" method, the system can consider various factors, such as a customer's spending habits, their location, and even the device they're using. This way, it can build a unique profile for each customer, making it easier to identify when something feels off. If a customer who usually makes small purchases suddenly tries to buy an expensive item from a different country, the system might flag that transaction for a closer look. This forward-thinking approach not only helps catch fraudulent transactions but also lowers the number of false alarms, ensuring that real customers aren't mistakenly marked as potential fraudsters.

The influence of AI and machine learning goes beyond just catching fraud; these technologies are also transforming customer experience in exciting ways. In our fast-paced world, customers want quick and easy transactions. Nobody enjoys getting held up by slow payment processes or complicated verification steps. By using AI, businesses can simplify their payment processes, making them faster and more user-friendly. AI-powered chatbots can assist customers in real-time, answering their questions about payments, helping them with issues, and even providing personalized suggestions based on their buying history.

Furthermore, AI can boost security measures without making the user experience cumbersome. For instance, biometric authentication methods—like facial recognition or fingerprint scanning—are becoming more common in payment systems. These methods provide a higher level of security compared to traditional passwords and offer a smoother experience for users. Just imagine authorizing a payment by simply glancing at your phone, rather than scrambling to remember a password or typing in a long verification code. This kind of convenience is a big draw for consumers who value both their time and their security.

Let's also explore the potential of predictive analytics in the payment space. By examining data trends and customer behavior, AI can predict future needs and preferences, allowing businesses to tailor their offerings. For instance, if a customer frequently buys coffee in the mornings, a payment app could send them a reminder or offer a discount on their favorite coffee drink at a nearby café. This not only improves the customer experience with personalized engagement but also encourages loyalty, as customers are more likely to return to businesses that understand and respond to their needs.

However, like any groundbreaking technology, there are challenges and ethical questions to consider. Relying on AI and machine learning raises concerns about data privacy and security. Customers need to trust that their data is being handled with care. Finding a balance between using data to enhance services and respecting user privacy is essential for maintaining confidence in the payment system. Businesses must be open about how they use customer data and invest in strong security measures to protect it.

Additionally, we cannot overlook the possibility of bias in machine learning algorithms. If the data used to train these algorithms is flawed, it can lead to biased results. For example, if a machine learning model is taught using historical transaction data that reflects existing biases, it might disadvantage certain groups of customers. Tackling these biases requires ongoing vigilance and collaboration between tech experts and ethicists to ensure fairness and inclusivity in how AI technologies are applied.

Looking ahead, it's clear that AI and machine learning will play a vital role in shaping the future of payment systems. By improving fraud detection and enhancing customer experience, these technologies are changing how we handle transactions. Businesses that welcome this innovation will not only gain a competitive advantage but will also build trust and loyalty with their customers. The road ahead is sure to be thrilling as we witness a transformation in how payments are processed, secured, and experienced.

In a time when technology is advancing at breakneck speed, the ability to adapt is crucial. Payment processors and financial institutions must stay alert and keep innovating, ensuring they make the most of AI and machine learning. As we navigate this evolving landscape, one thing is certain: the future of payments lies at the crossroads of security, convenience, and satisfaction, where technology and human connection come together to create a smooth financial experience.

The Internet of Things (IoT): Envisioning a World Where Your Fridge Can Reorder Milk

Imagine a lively household on a typical weekday morning: kids are finishing their breakfast, parents are rushing to get ready for work, and the kitchen is buzzing with activity. Amid the sound of clattering dishes and the delicious smell of brewing coffee, one common problem stands out—running out of milk. In a traditional scenario, this often means a frantic dash to the store, or worse, realizing you have to carve out time from your busy day for a quick grocery run. Now, picture a world where all this hassle simply disappears. That's where the Internet of Things (IoT) comes in—a groundbreaking idea that's changing how we interact with the everyday items around us, allowing your fridge to automatically reorder milk whenever you're running low.

At its heart, the Internet of Things refers to a huge network of connected devices that can talk to each other and share information. From smart thermostats that adjust to your comfort level to fitness trackers that keep tabs on your health, IoT gadgets are becoming a bigger part of our lives, making things easier and more efficient. This interconnectedness holds exciting possibilities for how we handle payments. With IoT, our everyday appliances can do more than just sit there; they can take action, gather information, and even handle transactions without us having to lift a finger.

Let's take a closer look at the smart fridge. Imagine a high-tech appliance that comes with sensors to keep an eye on what's inside. These sensors can track items like milk, eggs, and fresh fruits, sending alerts when supplies are running low. When the milk gets below a certain level, the fridge can automatically order more through an online grocery service. It's a straightforward yet powerful example of IoT in action. No more late-night trips to the store or last-minute texts to your partner asking them to pick up a gallon of milk on their way home. Your fridge does all the thinking for you, seamlessly fitting into your daily routine.

But this convenience is just the beginning. As IoT technology keeps growing, it's also changing how we think about payments. More and more smart appliances are being designed with the ability to make payments, allowing them to take care of transactions without needing human input. So when your fridge orders that milk, it can securely handle the payment through a digital wallet, making the whole process smooth and easy. This gives us a glimpse into a future where our homes not only respond to our needs but also manage our finances in real time.

Now, let's think about what this all means for how consumers behave. As our appliances become smarter and more independent, our views on spending and budgeting might change significantly. In this new world, buying things could become almost invisible. People might find themselves on autopilot, unaware of the many transactions happening behind the scenes. While this could make spending feel effortless, it also brings up important questions about how aware we are of our finances.

The ease that IoT devices offer could lead to overspending. If purchases happen automatically, consumers might lose touch with their spending habits, leading to surprise bills at the end of the month. It's easy to imagine a scenario where your fridge orders fancy cheese because it knows you like it, or your coffee maker signs you up for a monthly delivery of your favorite brew. While these conveniences can be wonderful, they might also chip away at our budgeting skills. It's crucial for consumers to stay alert, embracing the benefits of technology while keeping an eye on their spending habits.

On the positive side, IoT can encourage smart spending by providing insights into our buying patterns. Picture a smart home system that gathers data from all your devices, giving you a clear picture of your spending habits. By looking at trends, like how often you buy certain items or when you tend to order takeout, it can suggest recommendations just for you. This kind of feedback could empower people to make better financial choices.

However, as we dive deeper into the world of IoT, we can't ignore the importance of security. The very connectivity that makes life easier also makes devices attractive targets for cybercriminals. Each device linked to the internet is a potential entry point for hackers seeking to exploit weaknesses. The idea of a smart fridge getting hacked to place fake orders or leak personal information raises serious concerns about the safety of our private lives.

That's why strong cybersecurity measures are so critical. Makers of IoT devices must focus on security protocols to ensure that user data stays safe and that transactions happen through secure channels. Biometric authentication, such as facial recognition or fingerprint scanning, could further protect these transactions. Consumers also need to learn how to safeguard their smart devices, including regularly updating software, setting strong passwords, and being cautious of phishing scams that could compromise their networks.

Furthermore, we should also consider the ethical side of IoT technology. As smart devices collect data about our habits, preferences, and routines, there's a growing need for transparency in how this data is used. Consumers deserve to know how their information is collected, stored, and shared, ensuring they maintain control over their personal data. Finding a balance between innovation and privacy is key to building trust in these technologies.

The future of payments, driven by IoT innovations, has incredible potential, but it also brings responsibilities. As consumers embrace the wonders of smart technology, they need to be aware of how it affects their spending habits and security. The payment landscape is changing, with more automation and convenience, but it requires a partnership between consumers and tech providers to ensure a safe and responsible approach.

In this exciting new world, where even your refrigerator can make decisions for you, we stand on the brink of a new age of convenience. As our devices get smarter and our homes become more interconnected, the opportunities for innovative payment solutions are endless. Yet, with great power comes great responsibility. As we navigate these changes, being informed and aware will be crucial to truly enjoying the benefits of the Internet of Things. The journey ahead isn't just about technology; it's about adjusting to a new way of thinking about our homes, our spending, and our security in an increasingly connected world.

Preparing for What's Next: Staying Informed and Adapting to the Evolving Payment Landscape

As we find ourselves in a world buzzing with new technology, the payments landscape is changing faster than ever. With exciting developments in artificial intelligence, machine learning, and the Internet of Things, it's no surprise that consumers often feel both thrilled and a bit dazed by all that's happening around them. The real challenge isn't just figuring out what these changes are; it's also about discovering how to use them to our advantage. So, how can we gear up for what's ahead in the ever-changing payment world? The answer lies in staying informed and adapting to the waves of change that come and go.

The first step on this journey is realizing that knowledge is key. The more we know about the tools and technologies available to us—like mobile wallets, blockchain, or the latest apps—the better we can navigate this complex financial landscape. Think about it like this: sailing across a vast ocean without a map would be pretty daunting. That's how it feels to explore today's payment innovations without a solid understanding of what they mean. From contactless payments to cryptocurrencies, we need to keep our eyes peeled for trends, breakthroughs, and opportunities.

To stay in the loop, seek out trustworthy sources of information. Financial news websites, expert blogs, and educational platforms are gold mines of insights about the payment world. Some offer more than just headlines; they dive deep into how these technologies work, what they mean for us, and what might come next. Explore articles that explain how blockchain secures transactions or how machine learning helps catch fraud in real time. Joining webinars and virtual conferences can also be a valuable way to learn, letting you hear directly from industry experts about the changes shaping our financial landscape.

Social media can play an important role in this journey, too. Following thought leaders in financial technology on platforms like Twitter and LinkedIn can keep you updated with the latest information and analysis. Getting involved in online conversations can help deepen your understanding and give you a chance to ask questions about anything that seems confusing. Just remember to double-check the reliability of the information you come across, as misinformation can spread just as quickly as the truth.

Equipping yourself with knowledge is just the tip of the iceberg; the next step is to put that knowledge into action. As the payment landscape keeps evolving, we need to adjust our habits and attitudes accordingly. For example, if you haven't already, think about using mobile payment methods. With digital wallets like Apple Pay, Google Pay, and various banking apps on the rise, making transactions without cash or cards has never been simpler. These apps often include features that let you track your spending in real time, offering you valuable insights into your financial habits. Having your financial information at your fingertips can truly change the way you budget.

At the same time, being adaptable means being willing to try out new payment methods. Cryptocurrency has become a hot topic in recent years, with Bitcoin, Ethereum, and other digital currencies making their mark. While it might feel intimidating, taking the time to learn the basics of cryptocurrency can open doors for diversifying your financial portfolio. Look into how to safely set up a digital wallet and consider starting with small transactions to get comfortable with the process. Just remember to tread carefully and do thorough research before jumping into investments.

Alongside embracing new technologies, it's vital to take a good look at your financial habits and make adjustments where necessary. With the convenience of digital payments, many people find themselves spending more than they expected. The automatic nature of payments through IoT devices, subscription services, and easy checkout processes can lead to a disconnect from how much we're spending. To tackle this, think about creating a budget that reflects these new habits. Use budgeting apps that sync with your financial accounts to help you visualize your cash flow. These tools can be immensely helpful in keeping your finances on track.

Staying informed and adapting to the changing payment landscape also means being aware of the security risks linked to digital transactions. Every new advancement can bring vulnerabilities that bad actors might try to exploit. As consumers, we have an important role in protecting our financial information. Learn the best practices for online security—like creating strong passwords, enabling two-factor authentication, and regularly checking your accounts for any suspicious activity. Don't underestimate how crucial it is to be proactive; a few simple steps can go a long way in safeguarding your financial well-being.

Additionally, understanding the ethical side of technology is becoming more and more important. As we adopt smart devices and AI-driven payment systems, we need to be mindful of how our data is collected, used, and shared. Transparency isn't just a trendy term; it's a fundamental part of building trust between consumers and companies. Make it a habit to read the privacy policies for the apps and services you use, and don't hesitate to ask questions about how your data will be handled. Empowered consumers create a healthier relationship with technology, leading to better practices among providers.

Conclusion

As we close the final chapter of our exploration into the world of modern finance, take a moment to reflect on how far we've come. From understanding the basics of digital transactions to unraveling the complexities of blockchain technology, you've gained invaluable insights into the invisible mechanisms that power our financial world.

Remember when that simple coffee purchase seemed like magic? Now you understand the intricate dance of data, security protocols, and financial institutions that make it possible. You've peered behind the curtain and seen the wizards at work.

But this knowledge isn't just academic – it's practical. Armed with this understanding, you're now better equipped to navigate the financial landscape with confidence. You can make informed decisions about which payment methods to use, how to protect your financial data, and even how to leverage new technologies to your advantage.

As you step back into the world, see it with fresh eyes. Each transaction you make is a testament to the complex systems we've explored. Use your newfound knowledge to stay vigilant, make smarter choices, and perhaps even spot opportunities others might miss.

The financial world is ever-evolving, and your journey doesn't end here. Stay curious, keep learning, and remember – in the realm of finance, knowledge truly is power. So go forth, tap that phone, swipe that card, and do so with the confidence of someone who truly understands what happens behind the scenes.

Walter Bancroft

www.ingramcontent.com/pod-product-compliance
Lightning Source LLC
Chambersburg PA
CBHW052159220526
45471CB00004B/1733